"Alice Denham—writer/playmate/muse—has written a mystical memoir about the Mexican town of San Miguel, an artist community far from the maddening and very mundane crowd. Alice paints a stirring portrait of the impoverished natives, mingling, sometimes uneasily, among the norteamericanos. Her vignettes cover a motley group, including charming conmen, horny gringas, lazy hippies, brutal policía and lost souls searching for...something. A dynamic performance from a master storyteller. Prepare to be enchanted."

> —Dermot McEvoy
> author of *Our Lady of Greenwich Village*
> and *Terrible Angel*

"In her latest book, *Secrets of San Miguel,* Denham reveals the kind of insider stories that make tour guides shiver with glee and tourists plan their next trip.

"Borrachos in bars, stoners on cobblestones, amorous flings in the afternoon, of course, the occasional murder, Denham's *Secrets of San Miguel* sounds like a telenovela but reads like classic literature. You'll love it. I sure did."

> —Mark Saunders
> author of *Nobody Know the Spanish I Speak*

"Sexy transport, my favorite means of travel," says Alice Denham (author of *Sleeping with Bad Boys*) in her latest sexy travel memoir. I loved *Secrets of San Miguel*—how real people live, make art and love in exotic places. Funny and serious, it has a beautiful sense of place and real characters, the author being one of them."

> **—Lynda Schor**
> author of *The Body Parts Shop* and *Seduction*

"In *Secrets of San Miguel*, with its enticing romance-novel title, Alice Denham's mastery of descriptive powers, narrative drive and tonal variety enable her to carry out Joseph Conrad's imperative for the writer: 'to make you see.'"

> **—Jane Augustine**
> poet, author of *A Woman's Guide to Mountain Climbing*

Alice Denham's *Secrets of San Miguel* is a forty year memoir of Gringos with Mexicans. We are taken inside a parallel universe immensely enjoyable in its complex depiction of the manifold quirks of the human comedy about to unfold. In these worlds wild artists, intense writers as well as phonies of every sort share the space with the perpetual motion of varieties of sexual desire. We find straight love, not devoid of conflict and a bit of kink, homosexual and bisexual triangles. The range of generosity in family life rings true and touching."

> **—María Arrillaga**
> poet, author of *Flamingos en San Juan, Flamingos in Manhattan*

"Alice Denham is America's best-kept literary secret. With a style as spare as it is evocative, her work exemplifies the effortless rigor of true poetic genius. This long-awaited collection of short fiction confirms Denham's status as a literary treasure of the first order."

—**Michael J. Bowen**
film historian, NYU

"With the eye of both a reporter and a novelist, Alice Denham regales us with tales of writers, hippies, expats 'a mezclada of musicians, artists, antique smugglers, dope dealers, local teachers, and layabouts living on invisible incomes.' Her eye for detail and insight into human nature make her the perfect tour guide."

—**Steven Moore**
author of *The Novel: An Alternative History*
and *William Gaddis, A Critical Biography*

"In *Secrets of San Miguel* you find true and touching love, a friendly neighborhood murderer, skin-crawling evil and extreme nuttiness in the same paragraph. An express enthraller, a one-sitting book if there ever was one."

—**Jim Morris**
author of *The Devil's Secret Name*,
Bernal Díaz del Castillo Prize for his
Vietnam memoir, *War Story*

Other Books by Alice Denham:

Sleeping WIth Bad Boys:
Literary New York in the 1950s and 1960s

Nothing less than an eyewitness account of the unfolding
of an era. Denham's personal memories of key writers
segue into keen literary criticism, while her trials as a
woman author and model are firmly set against the feminist
movement of the Sixties.

—Wim Coleman, review in *Atención*

AMO, the Feminist Centerfold from Outer Space

Denham writes better about sex than anyone.

—*Ms.* magazine

My Darling From the Lions

When Miss Denham is being lyrical, she is capable of some
really incredible language

—*Sunday New York Times Book Review*

Alice also has written for *The New York Times, Village Voice,*
The Nation, Cosmopolitan, New York magazine, Playboy, The
Washingtonian, Publishers Weekly, Confrontation, Best of the
Missouri Review, Great Tales of City Dwellers, San Miguel
Review, Solamente en San Miguel, etc. She has taught creative
writing at Yale, Smith, University of Toronto, and John Jay
College of Criminal Justice.

ALICE DENHAM
is the author
of two novels,
My Darling From The Lions and
AMO, the Feminist Centerfold From Outer Space,
and the memoir
Sleeping With Bad Boys:
Literary New York In The 1950s-1960s.

"Wry, gossipy, apparently possessed of an
extraordinary memory and nobody's fool ...."

—Stacy D'Erasmo, *The New York Times,* 11/19/2006

Alice Denham is the only Playboy Playmate with a short
story in the same issue. Her story was made into a festival
prizewinning movie.

She is a founding member of the
National Organization for Women.

Secrets of
San Miguel

Secrets of
San Miguel

ALICE DENHAM

*Founded in 1542, medieval San Miguel became
a World Heritage Site in 2008.*

*On July 5, 2009 San Miguel de Allende elected
its first woman mayor, Lucy Nuñez.*

MADEIRA PRESS

CHAPEL HILL, NC

Madeira Press • www.madeirapress.com

The following stories have been previously published in slightly different forms:
    Confrontation literary journal of Long Island University:
        "My Last Mexican Romance"
        "Nuestra Señora de la Salud"
        "Expat Love"
        "La Casa de Serena"
    San Miguel Review anthology:
        "The Naked Gringa"
    Solamente en San Miguel anthology:
        "Long Ago in San Miguel"
    Atención newspaper:
        "Long Ago in San Miguel"

Publisher's Cataloging-in-Publication data
Denham, Alice.
    Secrets of San Miguel / Alice Denham.
    p. cm.
    ISBN 978-1935178286 (Trade edition: 978-1935178293)
1. Denham, Alice. 2. San Miguel de Allende (Mexico) --Social life and customs --Biography.
3. Americans --Mexico --Biography. 4. Writers --Mexico --Biography. I. Title.

F1210 .S43 2013
917.2/03/82 --dc23   Library of Congress Control Number: 2013936380

The tales in *Secrets of San Miguel* reveal forty years of gringos with Mexicans, 1968–2008. They are mostly true, fictionalized to be legally proper.—Alice Denham

Drowned in Madeira wine, two flies began to recover life.
——*Benjamin Franklin*

Dedicated to John "Brady" Mueller,
The Rev. John Denham,
Raymond and Leila Denham Starke.

Thanks to all of you at the San Miguel Literary Sala; San Miguel PEN; New York PEN Women's Literary Workshop; poet Angelo Verga, curator of Cornelia Street Café Literary Readings; Jonna Semeiks, editor, and Martin Tucker, editor emeritus of *Confrontation* literary journal of Long Island University; *San Miguel Review* short story anthology; *Solamente en San Miguel* anthology; *Atención,* San Miguel bilingual newspaper; Tim West, curator, Southern Historical Collection, UNC Chapel Hill; and especially with immense admiration to my innovative and skillful publishers, Pat Perrin and Wim Coleman of Madeira Press in Chapel Hill, NC. Special thanks to film historian Michael Bowen for photographing the cover painting of San Miguel by Carlos Vital.

Mil gracias to the amazing people of San Miguel de Allende, Mexico. *Tienes mi corazón.*

Contents

Preface

San Miguel was founded in 1542 by Franciscan Fray Juan de San Miguel, when he moved the Otomis and Chichimecs up from the *Cachinches* wetland to the water source spring, *El Chorro*. Otomi leader Conin, once baptized Hernando de Tapia, spread Catholicism by integrating it with clanging Indian dancing and nonstop drumming that celebrated the autumn equinox. Today that means fireworks and church bells at six AM, dancing with feather headdresses and ankle bells in the zócalo.

In 1810 Captain Ignacio Allende and his troops and Padre Hidalgo and his poor *campesinos* from nearby Dolores roared out of San Miguel, in the War for Independence from Spain. For their good work they were both beheaded and their heads hung from lampposts. Mexico won and became itself. In the 1930s San Miguel, Cradle of Independence, was declared a National Landmark town, where no industry is permitted and the arts flourish.

San Miguel lies on the *altiplano* one hundred sixty-six miles northwest of Mexico City. They say that till World War II vets on the GI bill came to study and teach at the two art schools, the

1

rich were starving on tortillas in their family *palacios*. Writers followed in the 1950-80s along with hippies, rich kids, and dopers. We came to explore a foreign land that seemed an unknown paradise, the wild west with gothic cathedrals and Spanish patios in Indian mountains. We had a pact that *no one* would write about it. Till 1980 when a parvenu wrote a travel piece for the *LA Times*, expats could live on twenty-five hundred dollars a year.

Charles Portis wrote *True Grit* in San Miguel, Vance Packard wrote *The Hidden Persuaders*, and Gary Jennings wrote *Aztec*. William Gaddis worked on *Carpenter's Gothic*. Jack Kerouac and the Beats dropped in to visit their boozy mentor, Neal Cassady. Hal Bennett, the Genet of black writers, wrote *Lord of Dark Places* in San Miguel, and Clifford Irving, fraudulent autobiographer of Howard Hughes, hung around. Olivia Cole moved here after starring in *Roots*. Pulitzer Prize winning poet W.D. Snodgrass wintered in town as did Donald Finkel and Constance Urdang. Beverly Donofrio came when *Riding in Cars with Boys* became a Drew Barrymore film. Mexican comedy star Cantinflas was born here and painter Diego Rivera in nearby Guanajuato. Muralist Alfredo Siguieros founded Bellas Artes, the national arts college.

Eduardo, *mi amigo* for twenty years, has gone from student with a school supply store to *contador* with an accounting business and three computer copying services. In 2008 Eduardo became City Treasurer. In 2009 Poncho, whom I've known since he was six, became Lucy's assistant mayor. Internet cafes are everywhere. There are weekly art openings and literary readings and writing workshops and a bilingual newspaper edited by an Australian, Suzanne. The head of the Biblioteca is Ali, a Moroccan, and the health spa is run by the Lims who are Asian.

Ultimately Spanish families married in with the Indians.

Because how many of *them* were there? The Otomis and Chichimecs were handsome, more so than the Spanish. The combination produced probably the best looking Mexicans in the country. Every family has white, brown, and beige members. There are a handful of whites at the top and the working class and campesinos are brown.

San Miguel's colonial architecture from a lost world makes it a place like no other. The powerful families take turns running the town.

Mexicans call San Miguel the prettiest town in Mexico.

Long Ago San Miguel

At the Mexican Government Tourist Office in Rockefeller Center, I glanced through a list of towns to spend the summer writing my first novel. I read to San Miguel de Allende—cool mountains—15,000 people—artists colony. It actually said that!

Breathlessly young, I bought a one-way ticket to Mexico City in the late Fifties. As we dipped through high white cumulus to land, I gasped, "Popo and Ixta." My favorite volcanoes from childhood jutted up snowy and magnificent to the south. "Look," I nudged my seatmate, in utter bliss.

"Where are you staying?" she asked. Thelma the school-teacher saved me. She asked me to be her roommate at Hotel Presidente on the Alameda. Greeting us atop the foyer stairs, in white suit and panama, was ex-Mayor O'Dwyer of New York, recently indicted and absconded. We met two Texans with a car and the four of us saw *everything*, from Bellas Artes to Ballet Folklórico to UNAM and Las Piedras, the colonia consisting of volcanic rock, to the floating gardens at Xochimilco. The Anthropology Museum did not yet exist.

Dining at the hotel, two American Embassy staffers asked where I was going. When I said San Miguel, they hooted, "The

5

Hepatitis capital of Mexico! Go to the Embassy and get a Gamma Globulin shot *before* you leave town." I did, and it saved me. The Hep B shot did not yet exist.

On the bus to Taxco, I saw thatched grass-roofed huts dotting the countryside, campesinos with comfy bare feet on dirt, chickens clucking, wash drying on bushes in the scrubby winding hills. In Taxco my hotel overlooked the square where buses parked so tourists could shop for silver. The first expatriot *pueblo*, Taxco was the silver capitol of Mexico.

I climbed the high hill behind town, past small family *casitas*, up and up I went. In a flat space at top were thirty or so pigs snuffling and two in the center were making out, pink on pink. The Mexican blue sky floated white shapely clouds, I sighed with delight. On the way down an old man ran out of his *casita* and aimed a silver pistol at me, hollering curses. His daughter came out and grabbed him.

I mapped out a route to San Miguel without returning to Mexico City—from Taxco to Ixtapan to Toluca to Querétaro to San Miguel. This ingenuity turned a one-day trip into two. By the time we reached Toluca at 5:30 PM, the San Miguel bus had just pulled out. I burst into tears. Two Mexican gentlemen in suits took pity and showed me to a hotel. "You can have a nice room and a nice dinner and start fresh tomorrow," they patted me and we shook hands.

"*Mil gracias, mil gracias, señores!*" I said.

Our rickety bus careened along the high green plateau with the Sierras gliding the horizon in curving *cordilleras*. We began the long steep dramatic drop down the cobblestones of the *Salida* into San Miguel. Grand carved stone *palacios* and crumbling adobe *casitas* sloped together incredibly down, further down than a single road can bump, and still further down the mountain, with steep streets falling off the side like stone waterfalls, and high paths leading to the clouds on the upside. Little chapels with bells, then a sharp turn into sloping Calle San Francisco, lurching down into town.

At the Hotel Vista Hermosa, José the proprietor played the guitar as his curvy wife, Ruth, served us. We dined at a huge communal wooden table, guests and local Mexicans and expats. We all helped ourselves from the huge soup bowl that dominated the table. Delicious soup—Mexicans have always made the world's best soup. It was that easy to get to know people.

San Miguel was totally black and silent at night. No streetlights, only three cars. Occasionally horses' hooves rang on cobblestones as a lone rider came through. I could hear my night visitor's boots clonk on the stones all the way up the hill. The tiny village stretched four blocks in every direction from the *Jardín*, the main square, guarded by the *Parroquia*, its gothic spikes spearing the mountain air.

From my French door balcony on the third floor of the Palomar *apartamientos*, we saw the entire town to the distant mountains. We watched separate rain sleeves over the distant blue Sierras. Rain slammed into town and cascaded down the sloping streets a foot high. Wherever you were, you stayed. Fernando stayed the night.

Fernando, my Otomi, was the first local swain to learn English. "I'm fighting in the *corrida* Sunday. May I invite you?" *Sí, sí, sí!* He'd fought since he was twelve. His friends called him Flamenco because he held his head high in a slightly formal manner.

What I liked about Fernando was that he was unlike anyone I'd ever known. Fernando had just graduated from UNAM

in architecture and was building his first commission in town.
That it was the local *bordello*, he would ever after deny.

"You remind me of the moon," I said because he possessed
that Indian stillness. "You say things to me no one else does," he
said. His somber face sometimes bore centuries of tragedy.

San Miguel felt like an oasis on the moon. We could see every
star. We could see the Milky Way. Waving corn fields stretched
into the *campo* on every side. I feared I'd wake up choked by
green *maíz*, smothering me in its green carpet. I'd never lived in
a place so small.

At the *corrida*, as the hero's girl, I preened. When Fernando
stopped in front of me to dedicate his bull, my heart soared. Fernando dedicated his bull to the señora I'd been chatting with,
who turned out to be movie star María Montoya. "I had to honor
the celebrity," said he. Later he confessed that he fought best at
fourteen, then he knew fear.

Day and night folks sat in the *Jardín*, the *zócalo*, amid flowers
and fountains, and a small gazebo bandstand, bordered by trees
clipped to twirling tutus. One side faced the *Parroquia* and the
opposite, the *cárcel* and *Presidencia*, the city hall. The other sides
were arched with *portales*. The one with outdoor food stands was
called Hepatitis Alley.

Sunday night *Paseo* in the *Jardín*, girls and boys swung past
each other, grackles bedded down in the trees, after their cocktail chirp, when who do I see but *mi novio*, Fernando, flirting
with a blonde, tall, pretty young *gringa*. He was smiling, courtly.

"Alicia, this is Trudy and Señora Vanderhuff, her *madre*, from
Long Island."

"Trudy is studying to be a museum curator," said *la madre*.

"Marvelous," I said, seething with jealousy, "I'm a writer, I
hope."

Later he told me he admired her devotedly because she was a virgin. She wouldn't sleep with him, like I did. I was a model with an MA and my first story published in prestigious *Discovery* literary review. SHE was a holy virgin. Fortunately for me, her holiness and mother left town three days later.

Next afternoon in town, a sight from the Middle Ages: wailing and moaning and thumping whips. Sweeping down Calle San Francisco were the *Flagellantes*, a hundred or so ragged devotees whipping themselves on the back and legs till they bled, on their yearly pilgrimage to their church at Atotonilco, to scourge themselves for their sins.

I was accidentally hit by a latecomer with his soggy lash. "Ow!" I hollered in surprise, not hurt. "O," he wailed, fell on his knees and beat himself on the back till I yelled, "No, no," helped him up and he loped along and hit himself in slow rhythm. Sadly, their real sin was poverty,

Many Mexicans were so poor they wore wrapped pants and rubber tire sandals wrapped with cloth. Women with babies swathed in old black-and-white *rebozos* looked too thin to cradle an infant. Poor Mexicans were hungry—no work, no skills, no such luxury as jeans and t-shirts. One evening at an outdoor café, a poor boy hovered watching me eat. When I pushed my plate aside, he rushed over and asked to have the rest. Cows and pigs and turkeys lived in town with the resident chickens and burros. When one was butchered, you rushed to get the meat. Butchers had no refrigeration.

The Mexican movie shooting in town starred María Montoya, directed by her American husband, Fred Wiseman. The Parador threw a big farewell party for the cast. *Novillero* José Torres invited me to go. We sat with movie star Eduardo Noriega and writer Carlos Fuentes. Fuentes, in his neophyte stage, was nosing around for movie scripts and hardly acting the great writer he became with *The Death of Artemio Cruz*. José wandered off and Carlos Fuentes saw me home. We were both politely uninterested.

Walking downhill one evening, I was offered a ride by Maestro Cruz, Fernando's master workman, in his broken-down coupe. Some men yelled to him and he stopped the car.

Three Indians ambled over and El Maestro greeted them with gurgles of laughter and embarrassed evasions like a twelve-year-old caught with a girl by his gang. He introduced me as A Friend, squirming about as two of the men reached in and pummeled his shoulder and pulled his sombrero down over his eyes. The other man came round to my side of the car and leaned his elbows on the door. His forearms reached into the car, hands dangling, and I had to lean toward the Maestro to keep his hand from touching my breast.

"Como estas, *guapa*?" the man said.

"Bien, gracias. Let's go, Maestro."

He waved off his friends and drove on, Cruz grinning like the cat that swallowed the hightoned canary. Men I barely knew presented me to their friends as their secret mistress. A *gringa* gave a man status.

The Maestro's face changed from victor to victim in a flash. "I like very much to take a *copa* with you in the Patio, but I cannot."

"Why not? I'm inviting—on me."

"Because, Señorita Alicia, you are high people and I am low people. It's not permitted for me to be alone in restaurant in your company. It's a matter of class."

"Class, class! Maestro, *I* don't care what people think."

He swerved to the curb and stopped the car by the dark post office.

He grabbed me in masonry arms and kissed me hard and soundly, cutting my lip with his sharp teeth. I spluttered and pushed at him but I couldn't move. Finally he let me go and I fell back against the car door on my side, gasping with shock. I tried to speak. Before I could, he opened the car door behind me and gave me a little shove, so that I rolled out of the car.

"Get out, *puta, chingada puta*—out of my car," he said frightened, and as I fell free of the car, he started it and gunned off.

I crashed to the cobblestones, bruising my leg and hip. A good thing I had on jeans and boots and poncho, or I'd have crunched bone. I dusted myself off then sat down on the high curb in a daze.

A man with sharply clicking heels rounded the corner and stopped. "Are you all right, Señorita?"

"Sí," I said in a low voice.

He paused a moment, shifting his shiny pointed shoes about, then went on.

After awhile I rose with a groan, aching all down one side. Limping slightly, I took a turn around the *Jardín*. I bumped into Maruja and Sylvia and we walked back to the Patio for supper. Fernando was in Querétaro with his family for a *corrida*.

Next morning a small brown señora with a baby slung on her back knocked loudly. I opened the door and the woman handed me a crumpled badly written note.

STA. ALICIA, you know who you are—
Do not think you can fool me. I am his wife. I

know that last night you were with my husband. This morning I go to the Church to see about taking you to the law. Maybe you do not know that we in Mexico have a law against Whores taking the men away from their wife that you be in jail for adultery. Watch out, you Never see my husband again or I kill you. Do not deny I have informations.

(signed) X The wife of MAESTRO CRUZ

I blinked at the Indian woman and burst out laughing. "Who gave you this?" Some *gringo* joker?

"La Señora del Maestro." The small brown señora was deadly serious.

"But that's ridiculous," I chuckled. "What does she think I did?"

"She know about you." The woman was passive and somber as death. "She say to tell you—kiiiiih," she drew her finger across her throat like a knife slitting it.

"You tell her I'll take her husband to the law for assault and battery," I said then remembered there was no such law in Mexico, for women. If a woman was attacked on the street, it was her fault for being out at night. I said, "Tell her to go to hell, por favor."

The woman went, "Kiiiiih—" again, like a machete lopping off denial.

I closed the door in her face. An hour later there was another knock, very timid and persistent. There at the door, hat in hand, was El Maestro. I slammed it, turned on my heel when I heard him wail, "Por favor, Señorita, por favor!"

I opened the door and glared.

Maestro Cruz dropped to his knees in the doorway. "Por favor, Señorita Alicia, I come to beg your forgiveness. I am very low people, it is true. I acted like animal." His eyes were cast down, sombrero held in both hands in front of him like an offering.

"Get up and stop that nonsense! You could've killed me, the way you pushed me out of that car." I stepped back, halfway expecting him to snarl now and lunge at my legs.

"I have too much shame for my actions. I acted like a dog. But you are a great lady, you will forgive me." He stayed resolutely on his knees. "If El Arqui know, he—"

"He'll fire you? I doubt it. Get up and look me in the eye, coward."

Reluctantly the Maestro stood up and glanced on all sides of me, occasionally darting his eyes toward me and instantly away.

"You must learn to respect people, yourself included," I said harshly.

"I do, I do—I have *too much* respect for you, Señorita Alicia."

"That's the problem, exactly." I told him about the earlier visitor and the note from his wife.

Cruz was furious enough to look me straight in the eye. "Which wife?" he said tightly.

"Which—are there two?"

"Yes, of course, my wife with the children and my *casa chica*. Which was it?"

"The note is signed only 'The wife of Maestro Cruz'. I handed it to him.

"What an insult!" he stormed. "I will beat up both to be certain, don't you worry. What an insult to a great lady like you. And to me—I am a *man, macho*—I do not accept insults!" A copper furnace glowed in his face.

"Well, try."

"What are you saying?"

"Just this," I glared at him haughtily, "you insulted me and you want my forgiveness. I will give it to you *only* if you forgive your wives. If you beat them, I will tell Fernando you attacked me."

"Por favor, no, Señorita Alicia. You will destroy my life." Sweat formed over his entire face. Even his black eyes seemed to sweat.

"*Pues*, is it agreed?"

Maestro Cruz wiped his entire face with his sleeve, ran his hand back through his thick hair and put on his sombrero. "You don't understand these wives, Señorita. They want me to beat them. Then they tell their friends that they catch their husband with a beautiful *gringa* and he beat them, and they are very proud." He shrugged squeamishly. "I don't really hurt them."

I glared. "All theatre, eh?"

"*Sí, no más.*"

"Like when you shoved me onto the street?"

"Oh no, that was a bad action." He bowed his head. "You say nothing to El Arqui?"

"You forgive your wives?"

He nodded.

"ÓK, nothing." I watched his face relax instantaneously.

I honored that. I never told Fernando.

My writing was going well, San Miguel astounded me daily. I forgot to count my money till I was down to sixty dollars. Barely enough for the *Aguila Azteca* and US trains to get me home to my family in Washington, DC.

Fernando *mi novio* and I passed the tequila on a tree stump at the station. We hugged and swore we'd miss each other unbearably. I jumped on second class and wrote poetry in Spanish and sobbed. Sadly I sang *No vale nada la vida…*

Daddy met me at Union Station and drove me to New York. My sublet had not moved out because, he said, he hoped we could live together. Now go, Ed, go, I said, and he kissed my hand, blushed, and left. Dad and I had a sherry. Welcome home, sweetheart, said Dad.

In the late fall Fernando flew to New York and used my studio as a crash pad while partying with her holiness, the virgin, and family on Long Island. The Long Island folks evidently said, Wonderful to see you, bye bye, as he returned crestfallen. My Otomi looked dark and dramatic in New York. What, I wondered, did he think he could offer a rich girl?

Summer of 1956 my short story was reprinted in *Playboy* and I became the July 1956 Playmate. Three publishers wrote asking if I was working on a novel. Summer of 1957 I had my first bout with cancer, caught early, so I had a cervical cone.

When I returned to San Miguel summer of 1958 I became the official girl friend for four months. I was deep into my novel, working well, and wanted calm. I went with Fernando's family to Morelia for Carlos Arruza's brilliant debut as a *rejoneador.* Fernando's oldest brother, twenty-five years older, drove the car packed with two brothers and *esposas*, a sister, and the two of us. That summer was Spanish. If a *gringo* spoke to me, I said *No hablo Inglés.*

Fernando, the youngest, lived with his old mother in the large dark family house. Out back was a huge open concrete space where he parked his construction trucks. As the first young architect of his generation, he was doing well and I was proud of him. Were we in love? Who knew? We were happy together. Though sexually I was the teacher and he the provincial resister.

He took me home to meet his mother, which I understood as an honor. Fernando was devoted to his mother. I was shocked that his mother was so tiny and dark and ancient. She smiled shyly and pressed my hand in hers and I marveled at how such a tiny lady could bear six big children. Her long dark dress and dark hair in a bun matched the old dark house. They kissed and hugged and she obviously adored and depended on her baby boy.

"I will never marry," Fernando said. "I must take care of my mother, my beloved *madre*."

We went to the Patio for *cena*. I looked around at everybody, waved to a few.

"Don't do that."

"What?"

"You look around at this one and that one. You are supposed to keep your eyes on me." He looked imperious and haughty.

"Why?"

"Because I am your *novio*."

"That's ridiculous, Fernando."

"I am very Flamenco, very formal." He posed for his portrait.

Chuckling, I got up and went over to chat with *amigos*.

We had great roaring parties. Fernando spent all day cooking spiked plum rum with peaches and mangoes. All his compadres and mine came and we swilled *ponche* and tequila and danced and ran around the apartment roof. We *gringas* had all the men because their sisters were not permitted to date. Only with a prospective *marido* approved by the family and accompanied by her brother.

After summers in Palo Alto and Europe, I returned in 1962. I rode with Fernando and family from Mexico City to San Miguel. I waited for him four hours at my hotel, finally got furious and absconded to the most expensive hotel, upon Atascadero Hill. Where I met a rich aristocratic Mexico City architect playboy torero Formula One racer.

I threw over Fernando for Lalo, spent two summers madly in love with Lalo in his hillside A-frame. Till I mentioned marriage and Lalo threw me over.

Fernando and Lalo were like most Mexican men. They often invited a buddy along when they were out with their *novia*. They talked with the buddy. When a table of *maridos* dined at the Fragua, the men talked and the women listened.

My Fifties and Sixties in Mexico, adventures on the learning curve of love. *Adelita que fuera con otro , Adelita que fuera mi amor,* I sang along with Miguel Aceves Mejia, read *Insurgent Mexico* by John Reed, read Octavio Paz, Neruda, Garcia Marquez, *Flowering Judas* by Katherine Anne Porter, the middleclass kid dreaming of revolutions past. I'd been branded. I'd been wounded. I'd entered another world. I knew I'd return.

My first novel was finished and my agent was showing it to publishers. New York became entrancing again.

Scalping of the Gringos

Across the *Jardín* sauntered Melissa, the young blonde hippie in fringed Indian vest, headband, and skirt. An Indian in wrapped pants and patched shirt gawked up at her as she passed, this tall child gringa. Melissa bumped the policeman's rifle. Tourists often bump the rifle because the *policía* stands at attention in front of the *cárcel* on a one-and-a-half foot flagstone sidewalk. Nothing was expected of these musical comedy cops.

Longhaired hippies sloped along San Miguel's medieval *calles*, boys in flared bells and girls in Indian garb. Hippies hitched, drove, flew in on their credit cards, and settled in. Craig almost didn't make it. Craig and Vanessa and I stood between cars on the puffing *Aguila Azteca* which crept from Nuevo Laredo.

Even though I wore my white suit, said Craig, who paid a hefty *mordida* for his long wavy blond hair. Mexico is unspoiled, said Craig, Mexico is paradise, Mexico is where it's happening.

I'm going, Vanessa replied, to talk to jailed druggies.

Whoa! said Craig. How come, Vanessa?

Law school project, U. of Texas.

Watch out, in paradise, I said.

As a woman, Vanessa got lucky being hired to co-write the Soap. With a man. She wrote the part of a woman lawyer. She became so involved she went to law school.

IPPIS INVADE MEXICO, screamed headlines in *Excelsior*. The tabloid *Hoy! Mexico* shrieked *IPPI REVOLUTIONARIES SWARM TO MEXICO*.

Heyday of the hippie, the new religion. The old religion, psychoanalysis, was waning but still powerful. In New York the International Forum for Psychoanalysis which included the APA—the American Psychoanalytic Association—decided to meet in Mexico City, so octupus-like had its tentacles become. The sublimity of this international body caused them to be designated official guests of Mexico.

Señora Graciela Vélez Lopez phoned the policía. *Jefe* Horatio, moaned Señora Graciela, I rented my lovely *casita* on Umaran to a charming pair of *Norteamericanos*, though scruffy, and within a week, four more lived there. I accepted three months rent. What can I do?

Graciela huffed to the Jardín, townsfolk accomodating Ippis on the ornamental iron benches. I'll go with you, I said. We marched directly to the *Presidencia*—the mayor's office—and she handed her *DENUNCIA* to the mayor's secretary. .

Along came half the original charming pair, her longhaired blonde tenant in Otomi garb. Containing her anger, Graciela nodded as she and I ducked into the cárcel.

Jefe Horatio, Graciela groaned, they eat seeds and nuts. They sleep in bags, the extra four. Yes, six now altogether. In my own *casita chiquita.* Their *basura* piles up—plátanos, frijole cans, granola bags. They don't eat. They don't wash.

I tried to explain the hippie phenomenon but nobody would listen.

Jefe Horatio heard this all over town. Ippis! Disgusting. Boys with girls' hair. Girls with boys' camisas and pantalones. And worst insult of all. Blonde girls, tall and fair, dressed in our local Otomi dress, with our tribal beads, our feathers.

He shook his head. Señora Graciela, *mi vieja amiga,* why do they let them cross the *frontera*? Has your *DENUNCIA* got to the *Presidente*?

I demanded he kick them out of the country! replied Graciela.

Bouncing on the cobblestones came two long black limousines. Horatio and Graciela and I stared. Can't be Ippis, opined Jefe. The limos swept around the Jardín and headed up the hill. In the Hotel Isabela bar in the Zona Rosa, APA members had leafed through brochures and listened to travel promoters. At last their tallest boldest member decided they'd visit that colonial gem, the landmark town that birthed the Revolution, San Miguel de Allende. Six APA members and families bustled out of their limos into Hotel Atascadero atop the highest hill. With its kidney-shaped pool and jai alai court, the Atascadero was considered the town's most elegant.

Señor Rinaldo Reyes Martinez swept in royally. Jefe, eight of these Ippis now live in my two bedrooms, in my very own place on *Cuna de Allende*. Ippis here to start revolution on the very street of our revolutionary hero, Ignacio Allende! Call the Federales!

Like the Chicago Convention last year? Jefe Horatio feared the Ippis might try to overthrow Mexico, as they had the U.S. last year. Jefe Horatio called the dread Federales.

I tried to convince him hippies were too stoned to fight a flea.

Federales in fierce uniforms and heavy boots swept into town. Rumors spread. Federales were here to round up Ippis and drive them to the border. Kick them out of Mexico. Long-hairs were rounded up and lectured at the *cárcel*. Lectured! Everybody laughed.

Didn't they know about Tlaltelolco, 1968? Mexico's very own police riot? Police massacred three hundred—some say a thousand—demonstrating students in the square of the technological college. Because Mexico wanted no disruptions during the '68 Olympics. The cover up lasted well past the Games. Of course, they didn't know Sally was in the women's cárcel for peddling dope, without paying off the cops. Her mother would, though—forty thousand dollars—to spring her after a year. Ippis loved Mexico.

We feel free here, Craig told me, arm around Melissa, his newfound girlfriend live-in at Graciela's. Lithesome, long shiny blonde hair like his.

I feel so totally Indian, said Melissa. Do you like my head-band—it's Hoichol beads, or is it Otomi? And the fringed vest?

Indians were In. But what about the Real Ones?

Craig laughed, Not to mention her rubber tire sandals. Know where we can score some grass, Alicia?

Try Roger Ripoff across the Jardín, I pointed.

Melissa pouted, I want—she held two fingers delicately to her nostrils and sniffed—*cocaína*.

You may luck out, I said, Roger's an entrepreneur. Be careful, you two.

Both gazed at me piteously and hooted.

Way ahead of themselves. Just like Ripoff, who got arrested a few years later. They ransacked his place, found no drugs, jailed him for six months anyway.

Paul leaned out and tried to pull me into the Cucaracha Bar, under the *portales* on the Jardín. The sacred Cuc, called One of the Ten Greatest Bars in the World by *Esquire* editor Rust Hills, when he needed a fast article to explain his overdue return to New York. Paul Rimstead, superstar columnist for the tabloid *Toronto Star*, has a six-month assignment to send back local color stories. *Copas para la casa*, Paul shouts, set 'em up. Pablo, Pablo, Pablo, they chant. Paul is the sort of roaring cantina wild gringo Mexican guys love. Arms around the campesinos talking *fútbol*. Bottomless pockets.

The *Cuc* was run by Chucho, the world's most beloved bartender, who let all foreigners run a tab and was never stiffed. High and low drank and stumbled between broken red leather sofas. In back was the wild *borracho* men's bar with a tile *pissoir* running along its front. Women were escorted past it to *Damas* upstairs and returned to safety by Chucho's *mesero*.

I'm the sort they never saw back then—a serious female novelist. *Por qué?* they'd ask. You're pretty, you can catch a husband.

Rimstead was writing a novel. Paul hung out in the Cuc and I pulled away and went home to write. And wonder if I'm a workaholic. You're no fun, Alicia, he says. True, when I'm working.

Vanessa and I talked with Sally in the women's jail, which was run by women jailers. Sally said she and her boyfriend had stumbled over Raul's established ring, that had police protection. They stole customers away. Now and then, said Sally, policía come over from the men's jail and threaten me because they want money, but they keep upping the amount. Every day her mother has to bring food, plus sheets and towels. In the cold stone cell, Sally shivers in a sweater, heavy sox. Sally's mother brought sweaters and sox for all fifteen women. They aren't so much mistreated as ignored. I bought three dozen enchiladas and dropped them off on my way home.

Home is Hotel Sautto where the tiarraed peacock struts, the codimundi rattles his chain, and the parrot sings *Pancho Panchito Toro*, as he's drunk. Indians cut the grass with machetes. The son, Ignacio, dates gringas. The daughter, Lucrecia , is not permitted to date.

Aren't you afraid? Lucrecia said. Your men about to walk on the moon?

Americans land on the moon. *Walk* on the moon.

Congratulations, Alicia, Ignacio said to me.

How proud you must be! Lucrecia said.

Till that moment, I wasn't aware it had anything to do with me. Yes, I *am* proud. I'm lucky to be a relatively well-treated American. I'm lucky to have published my first novel, in our late Sixties macho literary world.

I went with Vanessa to interview American druggies in Mexican jails for Law Review. In the men's cárcel Billy told us they'd gotten twenty thousand dollars out of his family to feed and clothe him for the past year and a half. As long as the family pays, he's a good guy, well treated. Billy has six months more to serve. In the Drunk Tank, slouched on the cold stone floor, were ten or so Indians. Buenas tardes, Señoritas, they said politely.

Later when I passed the primary school, on one side were a bunch of ten to twelve-year-old Indian girls, in those long wash dresses, gazing across the walk in awe and envy at higher class Mexican girls of the same age, with their pretty dresses, flashing ways, lithe voices. Sad little faces. Most would leave school after sixth grade, unable to read.

Paradise for some.

Sr. And Sra. Armando Gutierrez Arrillaga wail to Jefe Horatio, Seven, we have seven when we kindly rented to three. Rich kids pretending to be poor. What are they doing here? They don't work.

Do they save dollars and come, Alicia? Jefe asked me.

Ippis don't believe in work, I explained. They believe in something called Sponging.

Jefe Horatio explained that was *exactly* what they were doing. Jaime told me, he suddenly remembered.

Jaime is the black vet from Tenafly who married a *campesina*, taught school on the ranchos riding a burro to work. Older now, he's a cop and unofficial local greeter. He interviewed me for his cultural column in the Celaya paper.

IPPIS PLANNING REVOLUTION? shouted *El Sol de Bahio*, the Celaya paper, in the same issue.

Psychoanalysts and wives and sons in cutoffs and daughters in miniskirts swarmed all over, led by the tall pompous fellow, who breasted the group like a ship of state. His longhaired blond boy scuffled behind, both done up as cowboys. They dined at Posada Carmina, boozed at the Cucaracha, visited the famous art schools, Bellas Artes in its own huge nunnery, Instituto Allende in its family palace. As did every other human and bird, they hung out at the Jardín. Their watering hole and mine was the new Fragua, favorite of gringo artists and Mexicans, except the hardcore drinkers who spent the entire day at the Cuc. Only Diamond Lil, who looked like Mae West, was permitted to play in the men's poker game at the Cuc.

On the hot summer Saturday night of August 2, 1969, I watched the Presidente—the mayor—and Jefe Horatio get drunk together in the Fragua. Jefe Horatio had proposed a serious solution to the mayor for weeks. This Saturday night, watching Ippis cavort in the Fragua, once again Jefe Horatio begged the Mayor. For the longest time the Mayor said no. Till they both got totally bagged, out of it *borracho*.

When the Parroquia's massive bells bonged twelve noon on Sunday, August 3, it began.

That Sunday noon, Paul grabbed me and said, You won't believe what's happening in the Jardín. Come on.

A huge crowd was gathered in the Jardín. The crowd blocked the street in front of the jail. The policía were going wild. Two or three policía grabbed any male they saw with long hair and hauled him into the cárcel. Inside they chopped his hair off. Not neatly. With great whopping chops of lawn scissors and razors.

Stop it! we all yell. Stop the policía!

Twenty cops swarmed the Jardín, grabbing longhaired guys, hauling their arms behind their backs and marching them inside the jail. Young men emerged looking like scarecrows, embarrassed and angry and running to their friends. The policía sent longhaired Ray the painter running to the Instituto to get his instructor, Henry, to spare them both. When they returned, each was hauled in and clipped and mauled a bit. Both emerged looking like plucked chickens.

This is going too far, Señor Rinaldo said to me. They're out of control, replied Graciela. *Do* something!

Jefe Horatio was nowhere to be seen.

They grabbed and clipped kids. Mere fourteen-year-olds. Children, who emerged dazed.

Craig and Melissa appeared. Craig's long blond hair caused four cops to start dragging him along. Melissa pulled one arm and the cops the other.

Let him go, let him go, Melissa wailed. She hung on with all her strength. Help, Alicia! I grabbed Melissa's free arm to help her.

Suddenly two cops let go Craig and grabbed Melissa and hauled both into the cárcel. You, too, they said to Melissa, and pushed me away.

Oh no, not a *girl*, people wail.

They shaved the heads of two girls, possibly the only incidence of equal treatment in Mexico.

Can't you stop it? I yelled to *los ricos* leaning comfy against cars, in dark suits and Sunday sports shirts. How? they replied. Don't you lawyers have any authority? I bellowed. They shrugged.

Paul and I stared at each other.

Craig and Melissa came out of the jail, her lovely hair cut off into shreds, his the same, both with great bare shaved paths of skull. They were both weeping. Paul and I went over and hugged them.

Oh, Alicia, I've never been treated like that, sobbed Melissa.

Craig said, If only it'd been just me. They clutched, both shaking now.

Paul said, I'm phoning this to Toronto today.

Maybe we can get the American Embassy in Mexico City to do something, I said, still hugging her. This reminds me of Chicago,'68—the police riot.

Sure, protest, said Craig, after the fact. Like Chicago last year.

Two Chicano writers with Indian braids, José and Enrique, appeared. Stop this! they holler. Stop it, I screamed, now. Now!

The cops grinned, Come inside, amigos. They resisted till six cops hauled them in. Both got clipped.

Suddenly a commotion in the crowd lining *Calle* San Francisco going up from the Jardín. A huge man in cowboy duds—studded belt, high heel boots with spurs, great embroidered shirt and jeans—pushed people aside. A huge white man in a sombrero towering over the small brown townsfolk. Up close, those important masterful black eyes of a psychoanalyst. He elbowed people aside till they made a path downhill for him, shouting all the way.

I'M AN AMERICAN! he bellowed. I DEMAND MY RIGHTS. MY CIVIL RIGHTS. THE COPS SHAVED MY SON'S HEAD. MY 14-YEAR-OLD SON, THEY CHOPPED HIS HAIR OFF. WHAT RIGHT DO THEY HAVE? I'M AN AMERICAN! I DEMAND MY CIVIL RIGHTS.

So forceful was this immense fellow that the beige-skinned *altagente*, in their Sunday garb, scooted aside as he reached the street in front of the jail.

Arms and fists pumping the air, the huge man hollered at the cops assembled around him. WE'RE AT THE ATASCADERO. WE'RE GUESTS OF THE MEXICAN GOVERNMENT, YOU BASTARDS. I DEMAND AN EXPLANATION. I'M AN AMERICAN. YOU CAN'T DO THIS TO ME, TO MY SON. WE HAVE RIGHTS!

The small brown cops in front of him almost bowed before his grandeur. Humbled by this great white man. Obsequious sheepish grins. Meanwhile four policía behind him grabbed his arms, hauled them behind his back, and bum's rushed him into the cárcel.

People chuckled. Even I tittered.

Black hair shorn in ragged plots, like wild burnt stumps, scalp paths from the razor, it was not the same man who stumbled out of the cárcel. The humble frightened lowly expression on the psychoanalyst's face was one he'd probably never worn. His fancy sombrero was gone. Colleagues caught up with him and they clumped together commiserating. Turning power upside down, small brown had shown him his, and theirs. Their weakness, and his.

He got his comeuppance, I said to Paul. Helplessly, we smirked and crossed our arms.

Vayan, vayan a casa todos, the policía shouted at the crowd. Go home, clear the Jardín and street.

Curtain of Act III. People walked away grumbling. Paul phoned in his story, and ducked into the Cuc for the afternoon and evening. As usual, he tried to pull me in, and I went home to write this up.

San Miguel policía shaved twenty-four heads.

Many hippies left town. Many tourists left town. Paul and I said goodbye to Craig and Melissa who went back to college.

The angry psychoanalyst and the APA complained to the lethargic Embassy and wrote an article about it in the Sunday *New York Times*, August 10, 1969.

When the mayor was asked why this happened, he replied, I'm the mayor, I don't have to explain. Jefe Horatio lost his job.

The police riot united Mexicans with gringos in a temporary embrace. Slowly San Miguel became outwardly more civilized. Policía outrages from then on were against Mexicans, not foreigners. Foreigners only wanted to know San Miguel was paradise. It would be necessary for the citizens, now and then, to storm the Presidencia and the cárcel, as no one had done that day,

Five summers later, in 1974, when I was teaching fiction at the Toronto Writers Workshop, my second novel had just been published. It was a wild sci-fi about a feminist Centerfold from Outer Space, named AMO. I was on nighttime TV and all over the newspapers, thanks to Gerry, our director. Paul Rimstead wrote in his *Toronto Star* column about our San Miguel days. He wrote that I went to my room to write while he hung in the Cuc with his *compadres*. That I got published and his novel still limped along.

In 1979, not many summers later, raving roaring Paul died of his pure raucous joy in existence, of his own excesses, of alcoholism. He never finished his novel.

Vanessa phoned me to say she was now Assistant DA in San Antonio, some say the first woman in the job. At times, she chortled, they claim she's too lenient on smalltime druggies. I told her about Paul. We both miss that nut.

The Naked Gringa

*F*aye was relieved when the handsome salesman from Celaya didn't show for their date. His smell of wood smoke
and sweat had turned her on, but wasn't it a trifle high?

Three hours late Teófilo arrived, running on Mexican time.
Faye was at *cena* with Alicia, who actually bought a drawing. For
once in her overworked life, Faye was spending the entire summer painting and sketching, her declared true passions.

At the Mexican Government Tourist Office in Rockefeller
Center, Faye had glanced through a list of towns to spend the
summer painting. She read to San Miguel de Allende—cool
mountains—50,000 people—artist colony. Perfect! Her friend,
Alicia, was here in the late '60s then earlier this decade and now.
To celebrate Legal Abortion, she said. Alicia was a founder of
NOW. In San Miguel they called the Feminists *Comunistas,* for
two weeks, till they figured it out. That was scary, said Alicia. So
now it was Faye's turn.

Teófilo motioned from the terrace and finally Faye saw him.

Ornate San Miguel de Allende, once the villa of the silver
barons, made money off the middleclass yearning for wealth
it had never known. They bought mansions for twenty-five

thousand dollars and hired *criadas* for eight dollars a week. Alicia's and Faye's hotel cost ninety dollars a month including two meals. Half the painters and writers in town stayed there. Alicia called it the best deal in the Western hemisphere.

Celaya, though, was flat, dusty and provincial, a small industry town that nobody visited. Both places, of course, had their periphery defined by the hovels of the poor.

"La Blondie," Teófilo took her arm like a confidante, muttering about the last minute client who'd ordered two exhaust fans for his restaurant. "You look like," he laughed, "a fast Porsche." A vacation from responsibility.

"I'm a runner." Her boycut flicks of hair and long legs streaked around town, sweat pouring off her angular freckled face. Because of her fetish for fitness, Faye looked twenty at thirty-five. Because of the cobblestones, she ran on the highway.

Teófilo pointed to various freckles, "That's your dark soul popping out like stars."

Inhaling in anticipation, Faye decided, nevertheless, to resist the con of this musk ox with his teak skin and onyx hair. Some Mexican men are as finely carved as a church facade. Teófilo read a *béisbol* magazine on the woodbeamed terrace, while ambivalent Faye changed from the Guatemalan dress that made her look like an unmade bed into her sexiest pants and body shirt. Faye specialized in high fashion illustration, which she hated so she was going through a Fredericks of Hollywood phase.

"*Preciosa,*" Teófilo spun her around, "*alta moda in Mexico.*" Rich girls in Mexico wear pants tighter than flesh and seldom appear without cleavage mustered.

"Guess what I do for a living?" Faye smiled, walls covered with sketches and water colors, an oil on the easel and many stacked on the floor.

"*Dibujante, pintora.*" She handed him Sauza Hornitos as he examined the drawings closely. "*Impresionista,* like me. I sketch sports action. What do I do before?" He swung the *béisbol* magazine, watched the arcing ball, pocked it in one upheld glove.

"Out!" She grinned at this fascinating vendor of restaurant equipment, pool filters and cleaning products for hotels.

"Safe. I played baseball for Monterrey till I fractured my ankle. It never healed properly for me to play again. It was my whole life, baseball, since I was a boy. A little blow—*zas*—and no more. Now I have to sell things." Monterrey was part of the Mexican league where state winners play for the national title. It pays well and the best players, like Valenzuela, Orosco and Fernández, move up to the majors in the States. Mexico acts as a minor league tryout for the bigtime up North.

"What position?"

"*Primer base.* For four seasons."

"Were you famous?"

"A little."

"*Pobrecito, qué triste.*" Not to be able to do what had been your whole life. It would be as if Faye lost her hands.

Teófilo said, "I am learning humility."

In the palacio courtyard where they danced, Faye waved to *el grupo*—*Hola*, Blondie—Marlo on the ivories, Mexican guitar, Nigerian on congas, Lebanese Mexican Mustafa on horn, Alberto on base. Faye ran around with a *mezcla* of musicians, artists, antique smugglers, dope dealers, local teachers, and layabouts living on invisible incomes.

Faye told Teo he reminded her of César, the rich Colombian she fell for in New York. They all got away, according to Faye, who'd learned to leave fast. The melody soared up volcanic slopes with that tart hollow longing where their bodies centered and held. Even Latins who can't dance can dance; why can't American men sway?

The *Parroquia*, with its neo-gothic spires, jutted into the starry night like a pink iced missile. Teo and Faye linked arms so they wouldn't trip on the cobblestones. In the Jardín that day he'd watched her sketch Indians, tourists, families, deals. Her fast sketches were best.

Shy, back in her room, Teo reeled from the nuances of Faye's sophistication, not Latin at all, but more tough, more city. She didn't talk romance, she talked straight like hombres but flirted at the same moment. Faye lit a candle and they squeaked into leather thong chairs. She intimidated Teo, as the skyscrapers had, so he had Hornitos *doble*, and Faye drank right along. Gringas drank like men without getting *borracha*.

Teo stalled, ignoring his sex blossoming on its own. "How many brothers and sisters do you have, Fe?" Faye is spelled *Fe* in Spanish and means faith.

"One of each." Faye lit her second cigarette, her allowance for an evening out. Alone she never smoked.

"You live with them?"

"God, no. I'm in New York, Pris is in Florida, Mark in California, Mother and Dad are in Phoenix."

"Don't you miss your mamá and papá?"

"Not really," chuckled Faye and asked solicitously, "Do you live with yours?"

"Oh, *sí*. Two sisters *en casa*, and my parents and grandparents. We are seven."

"Seven! You're not married? Tell me true." Deft charmers, married men, so eager for dessert while single men inhabit a patisserie. Young in Manhattan, Faye once wasted a year on a broker, who shared a penthouse with three others, none of whose girlfriends knew *each man* was married in the suburbs.

"I'm engaged to marry," said Teófilo, "in two months."

"Oh? Well. That's honest." Faye always gave away the At Home outfits she illustrated for Bendel's and Bergdorf's, "to get into something comfortable" to seduce a shy man. Instead she said, "It's hot," and leaned over him to pour another drink.

"*Qué ojos*—" Inhaling sharply, Teo stopped her hand, led her to the bed.

"Yours are *diamantes morenos*." She loved being corny in Spanish.

Pleased, he took off his shirt, chest ridges like wood sculpture. "Your eyes—they burn," he said to be equally flattering and inventive, and she guffawed. Teo started to remove Fe's blouse with delicacy as she ripped it off and slung it on a chair. He felt dizzy, like a tourist in a strange land. Remembering Fifth Avenue, he said, "Why do so many Americans have dead eyes?"

"They're CIA, they don't show feeling." Faye winked, worked down the tight pants. She felt well dressed in bra and bikini panties.

"Like showing fear to a bull?" Teo tried to be as casual as Fe. Very muscular and thin but with some breast, unlike many gringas. Runner's legs, good waist. He'd never seen a naked gringa.

"Exactly."

"They are *muy* macho?"

"Some are."

"*Yo, no.*" To Teófilo, Mexican women were aprons or cloisters or sumptuous salons, but this gringa was a stripped-down racing car revving up. She didn't have feminine desire-to-please in her face. Teo bet she couldn't cook, paid with credit cards.

Teófilo was Faye's virgin. He'd only been with *mujeres públicas* and a sixteen-year-old *novia* when he was twenty-two. He'd never told anyone so she'd have reputation to marry. "Never have I touched her," he said about his bride-to-be.

Faye explored Teo's body as he tipped her *chichis*. She could tell he'd almost never been felt, his tender hard body, his body with its strong smell of wood smoke and sweat. "You think I'm horrible?" Faye whispered, as Teo flinched in delight.

"No, you know how to live."

Faye taught him how to use his mouth, guided his hand murmuring, "Gently, gently." He seemed grateful. "Oh, *sí*, ah *sí*, like this?" Finally he relaxed enough to contain himself and they began. "Slowly, slowly, so I can come," said Faye.

"Women don't come."

"Of course they do." 'deedy, 'deedy do, dove, with a little help from their friend, the fast learner. That melting sun bliss in the stony air made Faye orgasmic. Away from Manhattan, career, pressure, she was romantic.

Afterward, Teófilo was incredulous. "I didn't know," he popped his cheek, *estúpido* Teo. "You really enjoy?"

"*Sí, sí, sí.*"

"Gringas," he whistled, "a new world."

"Wait till the novelty becomes familiar, Teo." Faye never trusted the new to last. In her affairs, just as her passion blossomed, his always seemed to fade. Two months of summer romance was perfect timing for Faye.

Take her field—every season an arrogant New Look, not only couture but sketch line and copy pitches, to make last season mere dregs for the unchic, so that those who were With It would rush out to buy their new school uniforms for the year. People want change, not passion.

They visited the unfinished Siqueiros ceiling mural at Bellas Artes, the national art college with its immense patio garden and whirling arches, founded as a nunnery. They decided Sique-iros meant a warplane. They went to Romeo Tabuena's opening at the Instituto Allende, the private art school in its old family palace. Phillipino Romeo was famous for his overlapping color and shapes. They went to Danny Brennan's opening at Sylvia Samuelson's Galeria San Miguel. Danny came here to study on the GI Bill after the war. Sylvia's husband, Fred, taught Painting at the Instituto Allende. Danny Brennan sold a painting to the Rockefeller Institute.

Faye and Teo jogged together, they played catch, they walked the hills. Her large hands caught a ball skillfully. Teo liked her manner, not sensual like Latinas but confident, a breeze through his small world. A vacation from responsibility? They say gringas are easy. *Chihuahua*, you have to satisfy them or you go. You can't betray them; they're on to the next guy. They're not much for weeping.

Teo fooled her, hung in there, got better and happier. They invaded each other like savages sweating up crocodile rivers into sultry valleys, fluting in ecstasy. They learned one another.

"You've taught me what I want, Fe," said Teo, as they climbed the cactus hills. "If you come back next summer, I won't marry."

"What's that?" They were bringing a gift to a poor woman in a hill shack who'd sheltered them during a rainstorm.

"I told you I'm engaged to marry. My family very much wants me to marry. In November, Fe."

"So soon?" She'd forgotten.

Teo spun her to face him, "If you come back, I won't marry."

Faye had a fatal habit of not listening to serious declarations. When young, she hadn't wanted to hear them and as she grew older, she figured they were seldom meant. "But how can I tell what I'll be doing?" The floater to the family man.

The poor woman, Angelina, said she felt rich, sweeping her arm to the horizon rimmed with mountains, visible from her hill. Angelina's face: Faye arranged to paint her. Angelina's face had something in it Faye had never painted, seldom seen. Faye wasn't so sure she knew how to live at all. In her lap lay the valley, the blue Sierras of Guanajuato and effortless sky.

They saw *"Little Big Man"* dubbed in Spanish and Teo told her the words she missed, and she told him how it was really said in English. Teo took a dictionary to American movies but said Fe was an encyclopedia as well. They talked with Pancho the painter. Pancho drank too much, came too fast, communicated poorly, the kind of man Faye liked, who disappointed her early instead of later, so they became pals and that was the end of it. Teo didn't disappoint. Teo was apt, appreciative. He had a sweetness. He had such ease.

Faye could come back here and stay six months, a year, and paint and draw, as she'd always wanted to. She had the money. Faye couldn't bear to lose Teo, just toss him away, throw away art forever. But in six months she'd lose her career, her clients switched to others. Illustrators who walk away seldom get to waltz back; there's too much talent panting outside the door.

Faye was a slave to her own success. People came here to start anew, to try out a dream because the old one failed. Momentarily, Faye longed for failure, to be free. She felt happy here. *Como mango*, as she'd heard two businessmen say.

Happy—was an interesting idea. She loathed fashion illustration with passion, which was why she was good. Her cruel satirical sketches were called distinguished, which passed for snob appeal. She loathed classic sells, leather gloss, evening glitter, understated elegance, androgynous dressing, anorexic chic. Images, that's what she loathed because she knew exactly how to make them; how artificial they were and how insidious. She could be seduced by her own phony images. Witness her boy haircut.

Faye dreamed of sketching archeological finds, antiquities, of the leisure to discover new symbols painting slowly, constantly evolving. In Manhattan she was breathlessly involved in the Ongoing, currently, jackets for women with huge competitive shoulders. Her art, her seriousness, lived a halflife of yearning, an underfed child whose growth was stunted. Like her New York love life.

"If you don't love your fiancée," Faye asked, "you must desire her a lot?"

"No. Others, yes, but she—*no mucho*. Always at Mass," he pressed palms together, eyes to heaven forlornly, "praying, never going out on the streets."

"You can't marry without passion, Teo. You can find a vivacious sensual woman."

"I have, but she's a gringa *macha*." Teo fought the gut thrill of Fe's independence, her fire. "My family, her family, everybody wants us to marry. I'm thirty," he said with resignation, this handsome traveler for cooling and cleaning products. "Religion says marry or no sex. They're all so religious."

Faye felt sad about the deprivation of Mexican Catholic upbringing, how it limits individuals. "An arranged marriage, Teo?" That she could stop, if she dared.

"Once I'm married I can do what I want. I travel to Guadalajara, Mazatlan, Ciudad Juárez. She's a good girl, I can order her. Some Mexican wives say to their husbands, 'If you're unfaithful, I'll kill you.' Others, you say, 'I'm going out,' and they don't ask questions. You say, 'I was with friends,' and it's all right."

"Never with me. I'm a woman of passion."

"Never with you, *mi* Fe." He wouldn't beg. "Why haven't you married?"

"Because I want more adventure than one man and children provide." Faye hadn't changed her tune for ten years though she'd had more adventure than she could stomach.

"I have one life and I'm not giving it to anyone. Don't lose your life for your family," she caressed Teo's arm. "It belongs to you. All families try to possess their children's lives. Don't let them."

"Maybe I won't marry. Maybe I'll come to the States."

Silence from Faye. One word, and he'd be living with her.

Teófilo gave in, "Fe, stay and we'll live together. I have the money to support you. We'll marry or not, whatever you say."

Silence from Fe, and Teo felt sad about the deprivation of American materialistic upbringing, how it limits individuals. Fe taught passion but didn't trust passion. Couldn't Fe make a decision involving another? Did she make so much money she couldn't bear to leave it, or share it?

"I'm thinking it over," said Faye. My God, why not let him live with her in Manhattan—just a long visit—then return with him to Mexico and live together and paint and love, the two things she wanted most. In her grasp. Nobody would meet her plane at JFK. As usual, she'd walk past waiting families and friends and lovers and go to her empty SoHo loft alone. Nobody but clients awaited her. She'd have to go to the Lion's Head pub and scout out some action for the fall, when she couldn't hold out any longer. Teo, possessed by family, and Faye, alienated from it, which was worse?

"Take a chance, Fe. Don't be so conservative."

"Me?" laughed Faye. "I'm the least conservative person *you'll* ever meet."

Of course, he wasn't right for her, but had she ever had a man who was? Was she too jaded to trust Teo's love or her own? Romance to Faye was like her dream of Mérida, ladies and gents floating in white summery, whereas Mérida was dusty and full of fat Mayans in *huípiles*. Faye no longer trusted her own passion, yet without it, nothing changed in her life.

Romance meant summer escape. The blue bulbous sky out the plane window, Faye believed in that, and her career. Love was a vacation that ended. *Meaning* meant the challenge of competition, the mental titillation of skillful line. Faye was a better illustrator for being a frustrated artist, for never admitting she was only what she was.

In the Lion's Head in October Faye told her buddy, Alicia, about her great Mexican romance. She wondered if Teófilo really meant he wouldn't marry if she'd come back, or stay, or visit here or whatever.

They never mean what they say, Alicia knew from two summers with Lalo the playboy architect. "Those so-serious declarations just heat up the ardor, that's the purpose," Alicia declared.

"I see it!" said Faye.

Alicia grinned. There on the wall in a frame was the cover of her second novel, *AMO, The Feminist Centerfolk from Outer Space*. The Lion's Head literary wall held twenty or so recent books by denizens.

Faye returned to her conservative life of friendly Lion's Head sex, hard work, yearning to paint and draw and have real love. To her career, to her dreams.

They never meant it, of course. Though as winter passed to spring, Faye thought more and more about Teófilo, till she finally wrote she wanted to see him again. She waited till she was positive the longing she felt was for Teo. Not for anyone here in New York, nor strangers seen at twilight.

Teo wrote to thank her. "For six months," he said, "I suffered over losing you, Fe. I didn't marry because you made me want more than my fiancée. You showed me life. So I was more alone. Then a miracle. I met a strong passionate woman—like you—who wants me as much as I want her, so we plan to marry. A gringa too. Thank you for teaching me love. Teo."

The next man who walks in the door I'm going to say Yes to, Faye swore, weeping. Suddenly Faye saw faces of fat Mayans in *huípiles*, the smiles of acceptance, of easiness with life, the open loving smiles of San Miguel Mexicans.

She phoned Alicia, and wailed.

"You let him get away," said Alicia. "You're as stupid as I am." Alicia was remembering how she'd dumped Fernando for that rich pig, Lalo.

"I wasn't sure," Faye sobbed.

"Of course not, poor baby. Nobody ever is."

Several days later Teófilo phoned. "I couldn't do it. Two times now, Fe. I was seeing your double."

Faye felt dizzy. "But you got married?"

"No, Fe."

"Where are you, Teo? You sound like you're here."

"I'm here but I don't know where. At the airport."

"Teo, sit, and I'll come get you."

"Fe, I'm a big boy. Just give me directions."

"Why didn't you phone from Mexico?"

"Because, Fe, you cannot make up your mind."

Faye hated disruption of her tight schedule. She walked about the loft, furiously tidying up. Resentment and fear came over Faye. Principle of physics—infinite attraction at long range, revulsion when objects get close: in other words, protectiveness.

The last thing Faye wanted was to hook up with a small town Mexican. Teo had shown her his sketches. He was quite good, especially with movement. But the loft was too small, really. She could introduce him around. She might be able to get him work. Teo could draw. Faye felt an unexpected surge of power: she had something to offer. She'd let him stay a month.

Faye caught her own wild grin in the mirror. Her face heated with a giddiness she hadn't felt since her twenties.

Teo rang the bell.

In spite of herself, Faye was about to feel love.

Teófilo bounded into her SoHo studio just as if he'd seen her yesterday. Pecked her on the cheek, put his arm around her shoulder. The instant she felt his arm, she knew. Teo proceeded to walk her around to inspect her black-and-white illustrations, her new colorized, her paintings on two easels and stacked against the wall.

"This is you and me climbing the hill to the house of *la vieja*." Calmly.

"Yes," she said.

Oh, very absorbed, till Faye grabbed him by the neck and kissed him so ferociously she thought they'd drown.

With that, he picked her up shouting, "Ay ay ay," and raced to the bed. "I had to be sure, Fe," he said.

When his body slipped around hers, she knew she was home. He was hers, she was his. It was simple because it was so. Never never had she experienced that tart fluting volcanic longing *actually* meshing. Like a squirming yin grid had been perfectly melded into its yang. Her first series of surreal nudes began next day. Electric showers careening through intertwining bodies floating in space.

Teo brought with him a huge roll of drawings, some painted in long curving shapes, many sports action. The illustration world loves Latinos, Greeks, Italians, considered to possess more artistry that we ho-hum old Americans. Teo was a natural. It was easy to get him work.

Roger Ripoff

"Hey, *chica*, smoke, coke, whatcha want?"

I glanced up from *La Jornada*. Roger Ripoff. Vanessa and Faye had both found San Miguel, so now it wasn't just my secret hideaway. Faye won Teo. Vanessa had been elected assistant DA in San Antonio.

I swore I'd never go with a married man, another Catholic, or a drunk. Now I'd bundled them all into one corporate lawyer I was wild about in New York. But not wild enough to summer in New York. I was seeing Chema, a singer-comedian who appeared at El Arbol.

"You call it dope, I got hope," Ripoff whirled around in glee.

"Don't do that, *tonto*." In the center of the *Jardín*, the *zócalo*. On a bench, right across from *la cárcel, la policía*. "They're not deaf."

"They love me, I'm protected," Roger raved. "I'm from Mars, just dropping in on a visit." Flamboyant wildeyed, black curly hair, muscles, New Jersey roughneck sexy Ripoff.

"You think Jaime's your friend?"

There stood Jaime in his blue uniform silhouetted against the rose spires of the *Parroquia*, looking saintly amongst the rose and lavender flowers around the burbling fountains. Jaime the black American combat veteran who emigrated to Mexico after Vietnam. Married a *campesina* activist, has five kids. Small family, they want, he says.

I loved Jaime. He'd interviewed me on his local cultural program about my novel, *AMO,* and my ongoing research and writing about pre-Columbian goddesses, especially Coatlicue, powerful mother of the Aztec gods who created the One World. Therefore, Jaime and I agreed, *she, Coatlicue,* had herself deviously and cleverly created the One World. He showed my slides.

Proudly, Jaime told me about interviewing Charles Portis, who wrote *True Grit* in San Miguel, as well as Vance Packard who wrote *The Lonely Crowd* here. He knew Neal Cassady, famous for starring as Dean Moriarty, Jack Kerouac's hero in *On the Road,* his sole accomplishment in life beside charisma. Jack and *compadres* visited Neal and stuck their famous strung-out mugs into the Cuc and Fragua. Neal's old lady took care of him, as did many worn out Beat wives.

One drunken night Neal stumbled out of town on the railroad track and fell asleep. When Neal Cassady died on the track north of town, my buddy, Peter Olwyler, was called on to identify the body.

"Trying to recruit me, heh heh heh," ranted Ripoff.

"Wouldn't you look adorable in blue?"

Ripoff sat beside me, checking out my jewelry, I assumed. "You can't circle the *Jardín* asking everybody to buy dope. They're jailing dealers again."

He bent like to kiss me. "I'm clean, kid. *Nada en mi casa.*"

Shrugging, I went back to *La Jornada's* story about the popular *Narcocorridos* – drug songs. I taught Creative Writing to cops at John Jay College of Criminal Justice, part of the City University of New York. Vanessa and I both involved with the law, hm, weird. I still adored the cool air and open El Greco sky of San Miguel. I dove into my research.

I waved to English Anne, a gorgeous woman with a drinking problem and too much money. She was with her son and his buddy. She always dated her son's buddies. What was she carrying? Oh my God, the drunken parrot from Hotel Sautto. They ducked into the Cucaracha.

I charged into the Cuc to meet Gary Jennings, who was writing *Aztec*. Three *mozos* from the Sautto raced in to rescue the squawking parrot flying up and dashing into the chasing drunks. Among whom was Gary, writing *Aztec* when sober, which he wasn't today. Gary told me he was mugged at his own apartment door in New York, quit the ad agency, and moved here to write within a week. I liked Gary but I wasn't about to babysit a drunk. My corporate lawyer, Clint, was never drunk with me. Only at home, his brother said.

Roger Ripoff was no *amigo*. He was good at women and went after young *gringas* studying art and Spanish at the Instituto Allende. The Instituto was owned by former beauty queen, Nell Fernández, once Miss Kansas, and widow of the previous governor of the state. Every summer Nell hired George, who taught painting at Rice, to teach and be her lover. George was twenty years younger and Nell liked that.

When his girlfriends left to go home, Roger often held a garage sale of "things she left behind" or "stuff she asked me to get rid of." Not only old skirts and drawing paper and papier-mâché figures but also jewelry. Earrings, necklaces, bracelets, silver neckpieces you know she thought she packed.

I wouldn't touch the stuff.

"Look what I bought at Ripoff's sale Saturday," said English Anne, showing off a large carved silver belt buckle.

A week later *policía* pounded on Ripoff's door, led by Jaime, with a warrant, demanding to search for dope.

Ripoff ushered them in with a sweeping gesture. *"Mi casa es tu casa,"* said he, grinning broadly.

Roger danced around, following the three cops, chattering away to Jaime, as they searched high, low, and under, in and above and between everything in the house. Laundry basket, pockets of clothes, vases, *basura. Todo, todo, todo.*

No dope. No *cocaína*, no *marijuana*, no *heroína. Nada. Absolutamente nada.*

The *policía* conferred. The two *jóvenes* looked up to Jaime, who motioned with his head.

They grabbed Ripoff, hauled his arms behind him, slung on the cuffs before he even stopped smiling.

On the bench at the entrance to the *cárcel* a Mexican woman and a *gringa* examined the ten-twelve sweaters heaped up for sale. The sweaters the men's jail made for sale were thick wool in the traditional brown-black, gray and white. Wonderful warm sweaters everybody bought. Both women turned and stared as Ripoff was marched in. Roger looked longingly at the sweaters. He needed a new one.

At the cárcel they marched Ripoff into the torture room. One of the young cops patted the metal springs cot with leg holds, grinning at Roger, who looked terrified. Chuckling, they prodded him to *el jefe.*

"No drogas," swore Ripoff. "I don't know anything about drugs."

"You will tell us where they are," Jefe responded smoothly, "or we will entertain you."

"Cuánto por la mordida?" Ripoff took a chance.

"Ten thousand dollars, U.S., for the hearing," said Jefe. "An official fee," he glowered, *"no es mordida."*

Ripoff shrugged. He was a hand-to-mouth dealer. If he had ten grand, he'd be on Isla Mujeres.

At his hearing, which turned out to be free, the Judge sentenced Roger to six months in jail. The arcane subject of actually finding the drugs, he waved away.

Ripoff was amazed.

Policía marched him to the sewing room, the large interior patio where prisoners sat cross-legged on the stone floor and knitted sweaters.

"Macho men don't sew," he declared.

When they showed him the torture room again, he decided he'd learn.

"Siéntate," several prisoners introduced themselves, Gabriel, Miguel, La Víbora, El Ratón.

"Rogelio," he said.

La Víbora handed him yarn and needles. *"Mira lo que hacemos, Rogelio."*

Rogelio watched and they started him on a belt or sash, which he did very badly.

Gabriel and El Ratón laughed like crazy. La Víbora scowled and proceeded to teach Rogelio very slowly.

"When you can make a good belt, we will start you on a sleeve," he said kindly.

Restless, Rogelio got up to stretch and stroll around. The guard with the *pistola* motioned him to sit down.

Rogelio Ripoff sat and knitted. By the end of the day he'd made a decent wavery belt. The men patted him on the back. They showed him his bunk which turned out to be between the two loudest snorers. He followed the men to the kitchen for their evening meal of frijoles and tortillas.

Next day Rogelio settled beside La Víbora who was lanky and loose as a snake. The men greeted him and he knitted all day. The men seemed relaxed and the knitting kept them all very calm. Their *plática*—talk—was easy.

Mostly they were in for murder—their wives, *novias* when they caught them with another man, their wives' brothers who stole from them. Their lawyers, two of them had killed their thieving lawyers. Rogelio told them he was in for drugs and they asked if he had any.

"No, I wish I did."

"We got drugs," said El Ratón, "if you got *moneda*."

"Looks like I'm going clean," said Rogelio. He knitted slowly and carefully till at the end of the day he had a straight strong thick belt. He was proud of it.

By the second week the men promoted him to a sleeve. It took several more weeks before Rogelio's sleeves were accepted. By the end of a month he'd knitted a competent small child's sweater. He liked knitting. His needles began to fly.

After two months Rogelio made a good adult's sweater. The men congratulated him and La Víbora treated him to a *refresco*. Then Ripoff started a new sweater of his own design, mainly longer and slimmer with the belt attached to the center back. He phoned me to come see it and I brought along an order of *enchiladas rojas* and *dos toronjas.*

Next to me waiting in the *oficina* was a stunning young *Mexicana*, also wearing a wide brimmed sunhat. The matron took both our hats so we emerged into the sun blasted visitors' patio without protection. The rectangular patio had a concrete slab bench running its unshaded length.

Big families entered the patio and walked sedately toward their jailed member and everybody hugged and patted and kissed, grinning with joy and unveiling food for the family picnic. They had all surrendered cards, wallets, scarves, belts, pesos and packages. The men handed over all IDs, so they couldn't pass them over to a prisoner who'd then stroll on out.

Ripoff put his arms around both of us and introduced me to Magali, his new *novia*, whom he missed dreadfully in jail. How he got these willowy desirable women amazed me. Probably because of his rakish sexuality and snake-hipped gall. Magali's family had a rug weaving factory. She brought along colored yarn, thick and thin, in *rojo, morado, lila, rosa mexicana, verde, amarillo* as well as pure white and black-black to show Rogelio.

"*Sí, por Dios*, we'll do it." They grinned at each other and wheeled to face me. "When I get out, Magali and I plan to open a shop selling sweaters in my designs and her fabulous colors. Colors!"

"Yes, colors!" I agreed. "Why hasn't anybody thought of that?" Then I wondered, "Where's the money?"

"With *la hierba*, sweetie. *Un amigo*, Bobo, is handling my business."

"Bobo?" Bobo was a ruthless bigtime dealer. "You'll never see your money, *tonto.*"

To celebrate, Rogelio spoke quietly to a jailer, handed him money Magali brought, and arranged for a conjugal visit.

Once they were enclosed in the stone cubicle, with Magali straddling his lap, moving nicely, Rogelio proposed marriage. *Sí, sí, sí,* Magali yelped with joy.

Rogelio was surprised, just barely, that his good fortune was returning. He'd always led a charmed life—running dope, scooping up *chicas.* Ladies Man—he hated the phrase, loved the score, pure *adored* women. Cool tough tight fitting black garbed dude of the Western World. Remember when he wanted to be a playwright? The plays he wrote in college, where were they? His brain retired when he remembered such stuff. Now, this Magali was a catch, and he knew it.

In her family *fábrica* Magali wove on a huge old fashioned wooden loom with pedals. Magali's long nimble hands rowed her loom like a paddleboat. As she wove, she dreamed and planned her life with the *gringo guapo,* Rogelio. *Qué milagro* that he liked to weave, as she did. She caressed the strands like a harpist.

Magali knew she was naïve from working with the family and not in the outside world. But Rogelio liked to *weave,* so how could she *not* trust the handsome stranger? His touch, his *chile,* oh she trusted all of him. She and Alicia had become close but she resisted asking Alicia about him. And I, Alicia, resisted telling her. I was no longer with Chema. Now it was Francisco, the tall lanky Flamenco guitarist at La Mamacita. Francisco was a little wacky as some say I am.

After six months, Ripoff said *adiós* to many *compadres buenos,* especially La Víbora and El Ratón, whom he promised to hire when they got out.

At Rogelio's and Magali's big family wedding, I was a brides-maid there in the splendor of *Nuestra Señora de las Monjas*. Magali was elaborately beautiful, her family bemused, and Ripoff on his best behavior. Being artisans, Magali's family belonged to the small local middleclass. All classes, high to low, seemed to welcome foreigners as marriage partners for their young. *Gringos* were often surprised to discover that the family remained in control. The reception at their huge *rancho* in *el campo* even featured a gazebo for dancing. Francisco fast picked his Flamenco guitar as Magali and I stomped out the rhythm. Magali was madly in love with this nut case and I prayed he'd be worthy of her. Magali was *embarazada*, four months.

They opened their shop, *Lana Luja*, right off the Jardín and it was a huge success. Ripoff had four jail knitters working on inspired colors. They made long coats, vests, capes and sweater coats. I bought a sweater coat in lavender—*lila*—with red, white and black trim. As fast as they could hire knitters and make sweaters, they sold.

I also bought a beautiful hand-woven *tapete*, geometric and abstract, from Hermanos Hernandez, for my Village *sala*. My eight by ten purple, red, and yellow *tapete* cost sixty dollars including delivery.

Their twins were born, a girl and boy, a complete family. Their lovely life could not have been better. The family—a large old established local entourage—accepted him. How lucky it all turned out for this scoundrel.

Ripoff traveled to Las Vegas and Santa Fe to market their *Lana Luja* sweaters, got orders, and shipped. Each trip he stayed away longer. Magali stayed home with the twins and the young

criada, Susina, who cared for them. One day Magali spied Rogelio releasing Susina from an apparent steamy embrace.

Magali screamed, "You kissed her, you caressed her. You desire that young witch? I'll kill you both!"

They both denied it. They both ran. Magali fired Susina and
hired Leona, a middle-aged matron as *au pair*. Magali cried on
my shoulder, then went for a little trip, as I advised.

Next time Rogelio traveled to Las Vegas, Magali kissed him
goodbye with great cheeriness. Then the next day she flew to
Las Vegas and checked in at his hotel. She'd hardly cleared the
lobby when she saw him entering the bar with his arm around
a very young very blonde and curvy *chica*. Magali stood behind
an adobe pillar. Her dear *esposo* Rogelio was all over the blonde.
Whispering and licking her ear, scooping her breast, hand on
her pantihosed thigh.

Next day Magali visited the stores and outlets they serviced,
presented herself as *la Señora de Lana Luja* who'd handle orders
from now on. She flew home with orders next day, filled them,
and billed. The following day she filed for divorce. The business,
of course, was in her family's name, a reliable name to borrow
the needed start-up amount for the store. The money from *la
hierba* being handled by Ripoff's *amigo*, Bobo, had disappeared
with *el amigo*.

Magali changed locks on everything, put Rogelio's clothes
out on the sidewalk, and phoned *policía* to charge him with dealing dope again. She hired two guards to keep him from breaking into *Lana Luja*.

"*Lo sentimos*—we're sorry—Rogelio, *mano*," said the two cops
who hauled him back to the *cárcel*.

Magali's family was adamant. "Charge him, give him twenty years," they demanded.

The judge, weary of Rogelio Ripoff, had him deported, kicked out of Mexico, driven to the border, and handed over to U.S. Customs to do with as they chose.

Roger Ripoff had simply never developed the habit of keeping his hands off women.

Magali, down in the mouth, ran the family store, till she met a young Tarascan, *muy chulo y amable*, who came in seeking work. His grandfather, he bragged, had been a full-fledged Tarascan Indian *jefe, un gran cacique*. She hired him, married him without checking his record—Chuy was wanted for fraud in four states.

They had a little girl. Chuy was as handsome, reckless and sexy as Rogelio. Magali, *parece*, went for a particular type: dangerous.

My type: I was tired of variety. I missed Clint in New York.

But Magali got Chuy at the right time. He was ready to settle down. At least for awhile.

As for Ripoff, when he got out of jail in Texas a year later, he purloined papers from a fellow who resembled him. This man never traveled.

Ripoff headed for Peru where he now operates a whitewater raft boat on the Urubamba. He married the Inca widow who owns the operation and their little boy rides the raft with him.

Tiny Tales of the 1970s and 1980s

Mental Disability WWII Vets

*D*uring the war stationed in Alaska, Bob watched the military plane carrying his wife and two children for a visit crash on landing and burst into flame. Bob was never the same. Many mentally disabled settled in San Miguel because it was hospitable to drunks. Their veterans benefits married them to eligible *Mexicanas*. Bob Scott, the handsomest drunk, married beautiful resourceful Marisa and they had two boys. Everybody got Bob to fix their TV sets, his specialty.

On my way to an art opening, I had a long chat with Bob. The next morning he was dead. At about two AM he'd either fallen and broken his head or been hit on the head outside the Fragua. I ran to the hospital in disbelief and there were Bob's big feet sticking out of the sheet. He had two oblong purple bruises on his forehead.

Marisa said their boys wanted to go to the Marine Military Academy in Harlingen, Texas, which was headed by my cousin, George, retired Marine Flying Corps General. Cousin George got the boys in. Marisa moved to Harlingen with her boys and married another American, a Marine.

Señor Marlo

*I*n the '70s San Miguel had never heard jazz. Señor Marlo the Texas boozehound brought his best Mexico City conservatory students to San Miguel.

Marlo played Monk, Mustafa played Miles, Alberto was Casals combined with Dylan and Roberto banged away. The look on Mexican faces—awed, astounded, they had never heard such wild ranging rhythms, those fleeting caroming notes Marlo coaxed from the piano. Marlo and gang played at Mama Mia for years.

Marlo tried with several women but he could only make out with *Hornitos blanco*. One night performing at the piano, he slipped sideways to the floor and never got up, dead at forty-nine.

Shooting at the American Legion

*E*verybody hung out at the Legion in the early '80s because it had a fine bar, great hamburgers, and a rocking country band. Mexicans packed it on Wednesday for Bingo Night. Burt, retired CIA, and painter Tish, his lady, sat with Conchita and Tish cuddled Conchita's baby.

Slightly dotty Lou Breck, called the oldest vet in the service, sat at the bar next to painter David Taylor. Lou handed David a carved antique pistol that looked as old as he did. David assumed it was unloaded.

"Very nice," said David, whose finger barely touched the trigger. The bullet ricocheted off the ceiling into Tish, who died instantly. Conchita caught her baby.

Lou Breck left town for a month. No one was charged. Burt suffered horribly. David suffered guilt.

Burt was driving his van outside town when he was stopped by Federales. They pushed Burt out of the van and took off.

Possibly they were thieves in stolen uniforms but the police fondly did it too. A coffin for Tish was in the back. The 24-Hour Association buried her in another.

After a time, Burt got together with Foy, a tall Texan, who was the widow of the mayor of the dusty nearby village of Comonfort.

Shanghai and his Maid

Shanghai, retired Navy seaman, bought two houses when they were cheap. He rented one and lived in the other. He hired Lupita to be his maid and his mistress, a common arrangement which gave Lupita her own room. Middle-aged Lupita felt successful, indeed. Her older children visited and Shanghai put them through technical school.

Then Shanghai sent Lupita to the *Jardín* to scout for other younger *señoritas* to visit him. "He will pay you," Lupita assured them. Over the years she was able to please Shanghai by providing young and willing poor *criadas* like herself. Finally Shanghai got aged enough to settle down and he and Lupita married.

When Shanghai died, the American Legion gave him a festive funeral, Lupita in her fanciest gown weeping. Shanghai left both houses to Lupita, who became middleclass.

Héroe

O nce in this Mexican village there lived an idealistic young *manta* worker who dreamed of a better day. The *fábrica* produced fine sturdy manta cloth used for clothes and curtains. This made the owners very rich and the workers very poor. No other real jobs existed in the *pueblito* so the owners paid starvation wages.

In *El Norte* workers had unions, Estéban knew. Though he was twenty-seven, Estéban was the size of a fourteen-year-old altar boy, which he had been, because he could read. His brother wetbacking in Dallas sent him newspaper articles about AFL-CIO strikes for higher wages. Union members were rich—they could own cars, houses, boats. Estéban determined to start a union of manta workers. For six months or so he confided secretly to other *manteros* to see how big a group he could gather. To his surprise, they all cast their lot with him, whom they elected union leader.

Their list of demands was simple: a small increase in wages for all. The owners, of course, refused to meet with them. The owners recognized no union. With Estéban leading, they picketed before the office of the owners. Who were not there, who stayed away. After work one Saturday the brave Estéban led them to the family *palacio* where the owners lived, which resided on an entire square block of the village. Shouting, waving signs saying PAGA JUSTA, they marched back and forth before the palacio.

I, Alicia, stood there, arms crossed, watching them. Nobody ever demonstrated for anything in this place. I was with Yancy, my first Texan.

No one appeared. At work on Monday Estéban declared they could strike and close down the factory. Instead, the workers voted to march through the *zócalo* the following Saturday after work to rouse public sympathy. Go slowly, Estéban agreed, with their new union. Workers strutted their signs aloft and people in the *Jardín* cheered, *Vaya, vaya.* I cheered too, as did other gringos, all pro-union. The news of the demonstration appeared in *Atención,* the local bilingual newspaper.

Sunday evening Estéban climbed to the *Mirador* for the sunset, to plan their next move. Yancy and I passed him coming down from our weekly climb to the *Cruz del Pueblo* atop the highest hill. We walked the long steep steps that dropped down to the cobblestones of the *Salida.* Yancy, son of a Texas neurosurgeon, was working on being a Mountain Man.

I called out, *"Buena suerte a todos."*

"Gracias, gracias," he grinned and kept climbing the sloping *Salida* to the high flat lookout and sat on the railing. Nobody else was there. They wanted to do it right, they wanted to keep the sympathy of the people. Maybe two more Saturday demonstrations before the strike. Maybe they could get the teachers to march with them.

Suddenly four *policía* surrounded Estéban, accused him of dealing dope. They hauled him handcuffed into the one police car in town, slung him into a cell.

Estéban hollered he'd done nothing and they knew it. He shouted so loud the policía feared he could be heard in the *Jardín*. They gagged him, informed him he had to confess to save his life.

Confess you smuggle marijuana, *cocaína, heroína*, shouted the Federales, not the local cops. They removed Estéban's gag and he was silent. This went on for half an hour.

We found heroína in your pocket, two Federales told him. Estéban didn't speak.

Take him away, the Federales said in disgust. Make him confess.

Local policía hauled Estéban into the torture room in the center of the cárcel, away from the prisoners' dormitory. The prisoners got quiet to listen.

They forgot the gag and Estéban hollered when he saw the electrodes.

The policía bound the gag tightly around Estéban's mouth and head. They pushed him onto the metal cot and locked his arms and legs in the metal holds, spreading his legs. They yanked down his pants. In a businesslike manner, they attached the electrodes to his testicles. Then they turned them on.

A little jolt and Estéban jumped like a fish.

Confess! screamed *El Jefe*.

Another longer jolt and he jerked like he was pulling away from his body. Confess, confess, louder and louder, the policía bellowed. Another longer jolt and Estéban's face lost all its color. They removed the gag.

Now you'll confess, El Jefe informed Estéban.

Estéban died.

Of course, El Jefe explained to *El Presidente*—the mayor—it was a perfectly routine torture. Mistaking their intentions, Estéban had been rude enough to succumb.

The entire village gathered and blocked the road, walking to *el Panteón* to bury Estéban, his white coffin floating on shoulders. Yancy and Magali and I walked to el Panteón carrying flowers for his grave. His weeping family, his enraged friends, slowly they began to roar. Louder and louder they roared.

On the afternoon of his funeral, villagers honored Estéban, the latest of many brave Mexicans to confront reality. On the afternoon of his funeral, the villagers stormed the *Presidencia* and the cárcel and burned everything that would burn. They torched desks and tossed them down the marble stairway, swung hammers at pillars, slung burning chairs and files through the broken windows. The police swarmed from the cárcel, fleeing the villagers' wrath.

El Presidente and El Jefe escaped through old eighteenth century tunnels, built for that purpose, dressed as women.

The villagers' rage spent, life went on, as usual.

Nothing changed till the village went into real estate. By then the manta factory was closed. The rich became developers and hired the factory workers as *peones*. Their colonial palacios sold for incredible prices to foreigners impressed with crumbling arches and Moorish patios. *Las esposas* of the peones got jobs as *criadas*.

They say there's been no torture in the cárcel for eight-to-ten years, during the village's prosperous growth. Even though the prisoners might hear it and smell it.

Estéban's spirit lives in the stained glass dome of the old church, silently screaming for justice, say the townspeople, no longer villagers. Others claim his spirit underlies La Manta gated luxury villas, where his factory once stood. We have no heroes, the Mexican saying goes, only dead heroes.

My Last Mexican Romance

*B*rady was living with me because he was the only man who loved me. I couldn't stand him. Though I always went for younger men and he's that, by some years. Going round the bend from loneliness, hence Brady the Tex-ass buffoon. Yancy had introduced me to that peculiar brand, the Texan. Clint, the married lawyer, had gone home where he belonged. I, Alicia, had never lived with a man in New York. We'd lasted three months this time.

Brady the accountant was once a monk, almost a priest, but dropped out of Seminary into Brotherhood and out because of sex, of course, but also because he didn't want to spend the rest of his life telling people what to do. He wanted *me* to tell him what to do. What *I* wanted to do was my writing. I was deep into my book about the goddesses, which I call *Ancient Feminists*.

When we make love, I conjure Eloy the Spanish doctor in Torremolinos when that was a fishing village. We drank *Quitapenas*, feet on the brass rail. Casa Suecia had a cold shower. The Med was clean and rocked with fishing boats, glowing at night like sea stars. I conjure Timmie the English lord in his teeny bikini strumming Flamenco guitar. At the family place in Kent, my bed had a warmer under the cover at the foot, and Timmie snuck into my bedroom at midnight.

Then my buddy, Faye, offered me the house she and Teófilo had rented on Majorca, at Deya, where I could work on my book all summer. "Think Brady's too cornball?" I asked Faye. "Brady's adorable," said Faye, "this huge lunk loping after you while you boss him around." My lip flared, "You're bossy, too. Ask Teófilo." "I know it, Alicia," said Faye. "Brady's perfect, he's as crazy as you are. You're too old for toy boys." Hip wiggling away, I said, "I love my toys."

My last European romance, maybe it could change my life. Brady had to work, I was free for the summer. Intelligent wit, that's what I sought. Bit of flair, bit of cash, soignée—I mean adept at expressing himself. If Brady says cute once more, I think I'll shriek. Or tells his joke about not buying the Brooklyn Bridge because he doesn't do boroughs. I hadn't been to Europe since the dollar was good. Marry Mr. Soignée, live in Europe, finish my book. Not my worst idea.

Brady wasn't gloomy, I was exhilarated, as he drove me to JFK in the Little Jewel, his beat-up '71 Plymouth Duster. As we landed in Madrid, I longed for Eloy, married in Salamanca fifteen years ago. When we landed in Palma, anxiety hit me. I didn't know a living soul in Deya.

Brady was half bald and had eyes like a child. Only good men look that way: revolting. We met in San Miguel. I first saw him in a battered sombrero examining a crooked walking stick. Who's that old dude with the beard? I wondered. When he looked up, his face was so young I laughed and motioned him over. I invited him to *comida* at our hotel, where we artists stayed at the best deal in the Western World which was set in a garden. Everything in San Miguel was cheap.

When he joined the table he looked older and less interesting, awkward from intense insecurity. His face had closed down and he shrugged involuntarily a lot, as if his long limbed life were too much for him to handle. Boring, I thought, borrrrring. Countrified.

Courtly, though. He walked me to my room on the terraza, invited me for a long hike up the *montaña* to the *Tres Cruces* tomorrow. As he walked away, tall, arms and legs flailing out like a frisky pony, huge feet pointing east and west, I couldn't help smiling. Fine body but his shoulders hunched in. Beaten down by life, poor fellow. No longer a priest or a monk, an accountant. Never in my life had I stooped to an accountant, the one profession women joked about—back then—and avoided: square, pale, humorless.

Atop the *montaña* we sat on a log and shared the valley dipping to the rolling blue Sierras sweeping to the West. We split a cool *Dos Equis* and Brady tried to feel my tit. "You're sticking 'em out at me," he said. I, Alicia, do that?

Stretched out on my bed, he looked like the Laocoon with his auburn genitals in the air, at ease milord, just as if he were desirable. I resented the beauty of his body which made it impossible to dismiss him.

"From the time I was a boy, only two things interested me— sex and theology."

"Conflict at the heart of life," said I. Good calf muscles just slay me.

"Not necessarily," said he. "The body and the meaning, the theoretical. I never cared much about money."

"Me, either. The search itself, that's what's fun." Epistemology, my favorite in college. "Existentialism became Freudian revisionism, then linguistics, feminist psychology, semiotics, now it's structuralism and brain research. Love it, love it all." I was reading *Origin of Consciousness*, examining the possessed state of the Delphic Oracle.

Clutching his virginity in his hand till age thirty, Brady was now a sexual teenager. His silky stalk felt years younger than his age. For the first six months I knew him, it flew aloft whenever he was naked.

"Stop acting like I love you—because I don't." I sloughed him off my shoulders, out of my hair.

"For a long time," replied Brady, "I wouldn't go out with anybody who'd go out with me."

Brady tried to straighten up but forgot out of playfulness. He'd lost so much he had no fear of losing, whereas I'd lost so much I'd turned cynical. But I was cynical at twelve, a non-believer. Ask Leila and John, my siblings. (I hate that word.) "How can you believe in God?" I asked him.

"Look at you, how can you believe in literature?" I understood perfectibility; that was art. I swam a half mile every day while he float kicked along. I understood why things didn't work; he just kept floating.

Brady fixed Thanksgiving dinner with Faye and Teófilo and we served six of our friends. Since his is a moveable skill, Brady began working a couple of months in New York then when I got up to here with him and started yelling, he'd go back to Houston and work there three or four months.

Not long ago Faye told me, "If you want to be happy, always choose a man who loves you more than you love him."

"I just turned over the Old Man," said the young man. The old man, Robert Graves, novelist and poet, had moved thirty-some years ago to Deya, island of Diana, the White Goddess, whose worship he wrote about; a major goddess who stars in my ongoing book. Graves, who knew the real gods were women, was trailed by younger artists seeking cheap paradise and each other. The Old Man was bedridden and had to be turned over again at midnight, said the young man. "Fortunately he sleeps most of the time."

I had hoped to meet Robert Graves. "Sorry," said the young man. "It's too late for that."

Stone houses with shutters closed against the vicious heat on the drought-ridden cliff the Moors had terraced a thousand years ago. Restaurant and disco on the very floor beneath Faye's so-called house in the center of town. Bikes roared up the hill and revved like barking dogs in groups in front.

In the terrace bar I met two men I liked who liked me, both married. One looked like my old Mexican lover, Lalo, the playboy architect, and turned out to be a German orthodontist. The other, an English psychiatrist, looked like a potato farmer and had a wife with a title. Everybody bought me brandy which was cheap. We sat outside at round tables in the terrific heat, one hundred six degrees at midnight, and drank till four AM when it was possible, perhaps, to sleep.

One hundred twenty degrees scorched the day. Deya's ghostly sun peered through the dust of the burning Sirocco. The heat made me ill. In less than a week I flew home on Iberia. The married English psychiatrist had wafted me a brandy, leaned over me and said, "You have those bad Botticelli looks that fascinate me."

A line Father Brady doesn't even understand. But there he is in New York—virile, available, loving me, unmarried, in my apartment, my life, now appreciated. That didn't mean I planned to waste my summer in the city. "My life is a gift to you," says Poppa B., who says beautiful things. But I don't let him get away with it. "Then what am I, you turkey, a taker? What about my life?"

We play Junie and Mistress. "You're my personal attendant, Junie." Hosed to the knee, buckled shoes, britches, jacket. "I get to torture you all I want."

"I'm a good boy, Miz Alicia, I do everything you tell me. Don' hit, don' hit." Presenting his rump.

"Your knee britches are soiled, Junie." She sideswipes his rump with her tiny foot then buffets his shoulder and swaddles his neck in a lock grip, which he permits like a friendly dog. "You misbehave, Junie. Kiss my feet."

She falls back on the sofa and Junie kisses all over each foot. "Mistress Alicia, I am your slave for life. Are your foots happy?"

Chortling, Alicia rose from the sofa and yanked him into the bedroom. The Domination of the Weak, Junie, I watch for it.

So, as usual, I flew off to Mexico where Big Foot Brady would join me later. The hot sensation in town was Clifford Irving, convicted of accepting six hundred thousand dollars from publishers for his fraudulent autobiography of Howard Hughes. After jail, Cliff and kids and new gal fled back to San Miguel.

I read from *Ancient Feminists* at novelist Bob Somerlott's Writing class at Instituto Allende. Gary Jennings still wanted me to keep his head in *Aztec* and out of the bottle, but I'm no devotee. Do I secretly want to dispose of love dreams in order to Give In to loving the only man I have?

"Does he have good character?" my father had asked.

"Twice as good as mine," I said.

My father, the Commerce Department lawyer and my mother, the pastoral counselor, liked him, of course. "An unpretentious man, like me," said Dad.

No fancy love in Deya, none in San Miguel. Dear Poppa B., dear Big Foot. I look at my aging arms in delight. It means I can finally give in to love—must—or lose out entirely. I am appalled at the plainness of my choice. I am appalled that I went for a good man like my father. I'm a sophisticated professor and high lifer. "Virtue," said Cynthia Ozick, "it ravishes me."

Then my last European romance appeared. The jeans and jacket looked more willed than natural. French? Chin beard, black intent eyes and curly black halo of hair, soignée, worldly experience in his eyes, face muscles, the fine concavity beneath his cheekbones. Not Mexican, German tall. About forty and very noticeable, the women noticed. He turned and walked backward staring at me down Calle Loreto. Perfect, too perfect, the man I'd gone to Europe to meet sat on a bench at the Mexican hotel pool.

"You're getting fat," I said, settling beside him.

"I know." He sucked in casually. "You're not."

"Actually, I am, but I fight it daily."

"How?"

"Race you." We dove in and I beat him across the pool and back. "That's how."

Leaping up, he ducked me and I came up laughing with my arms round his neck.

"Sasha," said a voice. An ex-student, Dick, recognized Sasha from his teaching days at Berkeley. Sasha was an Israeli anthropologist who'd taken a walk on the conference in Mexico City and come to the place they said was most like the Greek Islands. Cobblestones, domes and spires, high mountain backdrop, adobe houses pitching up steep streets, green shade courtyards, small dark people, tourists: very like. Vast green valley like the wine dark Aegean, for viewing, as we burbled through the painted cerulean blue of the hotel pool.

About the same time in New York, Brady gave up trying to phone—circuits were busy—and sent a telegram saying he was on his way to San Miguel, that he got time off work much sooner than expected. This telegram didn't reach me.

That night Sasha and I heard the *Catedral Nacional* boys' choir in the Parroquia. Way up high the boys sang in the stone carved choir loft, in belled niches for four, and Juliet balconies for two, lost boy tones echoing in the gothic empyrean and slithering down stone vine pillars. Our hands gripped.

At *Laberintos* we danced our Mediterranean romance beneath the disco's multiple arches, striped like the mosque at Cordoba. I drank tequila with Sangrita; Sasha, seltzer with lime. Sasha was separated, grown daughter, devoted to Israel. American wife "never bothered to learn Hebrew."

At Laberintos we fit. Our understanding of life undulated in our mature bodies, subtly suggestive with the Latin beat, teasing the disco, mellowed by the years. Two old make out artists, a bit ragged at the edges, made for each other. Hotsy blast lighting beat on and off: you're here, you're gone, you're up, you're down, you're in, you're out, you're hot, you're not.

"My wife made me feel I was oppressing her," said Sasha. "I told her to get a real job as an editor. She researches and writes for a famous psychologist, who gives her no credit and she does it all. I told her he's a surrogate sexist husband. She says she feels loyal to him. For what? Low pay, no credit?" What about me? Sasha wanted to know.

"I live with a man I'm very fond of , and we get along well, but—" I wanted passion. "I was lonely. Tired of going out to dinner and being alone for everything real."

Sasha's hand covered mine. "When I drive home at dusk, I get depressed because when I get to my empty apartment, I eat alone. Nobody. No family. Silence. At first I went to various hangouts and they were all kids my daughter's age. I felt foolish."

Everything in common. A three-day romance is no holds barred because no bonds forthcoming. Arms around, back to the hotel. A three-day romance is a free fall through space. Logically, but everybody looks for that irresistible force that wipes out previous existence. I told him what the English psychiatrist had said about my bad Botticelli face, and Sasha agreed, as we snuck surreptitiously into the hotel garden. The hotel family knew Brady as my *viejito*.

Smell the night blooming bells, roses, jasmine, calla lilies taller than I am, floppy banana leaves brushing us so we jumped, towering jacaranda and willow then a circle of true black above the garden where we saw the Milky Way, true marvel truly visible. We tippy toed up the tile stairway to my room. We lit a candle and had *rompope*, Mexican eggnog.

Everything in common including bikini underwear and summers off. In bed Sasha was so—gratefully loving. Expert as well, nuanced. Everything felt good and sexy. Sexy travel, my favorite means of transport.

Except it wasn't Brady. I didn't know till now I loved the way Brady smelled. Texture of his skin. Feel of his weight. His long fingered silky hands, flaring fingers, muscles, breath. Was it possible Brady had, just physically now, a better body than the well formed muscled Sasha? Or did I simply feel guilt, misplaced loyalty like Sasha's wife toward her boss? Brady swam around me, trying to get in on the action. Floating like Adam, trying to make contact with God's finger. What was he up to, damn Catholic monk?

Father Brady the Stripper, remember when we pulled that on the painters in the Fragua? Father Brady strides the stage opening and closing his long black vestments, his tall blue white uncrucified body now seen, now not. Swirling his robe, ethereally unaware, only too aware of his nakedness, spinning and whirling. They bought it.

Go away, Brady, take off. Jealousy's not my style. Guilt does not become me. I, Alicia, rolled and kissed with Sasha, my match.

Sasha was carried away, he was natural, he was the way I'd been before. But I felt deliberate. He plummeted my throat like I did Brady's with my arm muscle of a tongue. I liked the way Brady kissed my breasts, hard but not too hard, on the intense exciting line of fear without crossing it. Sasha kissed my various intriguing parts not quite the same way. But Sasha was marvelous. He lasted much longer than Brady but I couldn't come. Why not? The second time I faked it, annoyed at my body.

Since I'd met Brady, even when I despised him in an indifferent way, jerk wimp creep in my estimation—I couldn't come with anybody else. Never had I ever been unable to come with more than one man, oh, since my first and only great love of youth. It mystified me. I didn't want to settle with that goody-goody, even if my body had decided to. Why? Exhaustion or attraction? Probably both, like a stubborn old dog that sits and won't budge again.

Or did I resent Brady pushing me to birth, to calve like a glacier into free flowing love, when the ice block had almost become permafrost, so solid I couldn't even feel it?

That noon Brady flew to Mexico City, and hopped on the second class bus for San Miguel, the flying *Flecha Amarilla* whose motto is, Better Dead Than Late. He had tried to phone from the airport to make sure the coast was clear, the bed empty, because Big Foot Brady was cognizant of my peccadilloes.

That afternoon, our last, Sasha and I stood close and nostalgic at a small mosaic corner fountain that said, *DIOS NOS BENDIGA CON SU AGUA PURA QUE VIENE DE SU TIERRA ETERNA*, etc., which Sasha read to me in a soft voice. We went to Maruja Garay's opening and home to my room to bed.

"I know why I came here," said Sasha. "To spend time with someone who doesn't make me feel like a monster. Someone as nice and wonderful as you."

When we made love that night, I prayed my body would change its mind.

Unbeknownst to me, that evening while Sasha and I were in town, Brady arrived at the hotel. Being polite and cautious, he'd loped in his new non-Nikes along the terrace to my room and knocked. Got no response, ate *cena*, knocked an hour later. Then resigned himself to my being out for the evening, and checked into a room.

The next morning Sasha and I kissed goodbye, making plans to see each other in November if he came to the U.S. His university encouraged faculty to use travel stipends, imagine. We talked about spending time together next summer, wondering if we would. I could research Mesopotamian goddesses. But didn't our polite voices mean we'd both had all we wanted, and we knew it?

Now that it was morning, Big Foot Brady, size thirteen pointing east, size thirteen pointing west, loped along the terrace once more to my room in his new non-Nikes, beard grown unruly in my absence. Knocked almost, then heard voices, mine and Sasha's. Brady went to the window, wondering if he had the right room or if I'd moved.

And he saw my arms on Sasha's shoulders, his around my waist, and we saw wild bearded Brady, startled interloper.

"Brady!" I yelped.

Brady didn't know Sasha and I were kissing goodbye. Brady didn't know Sasha and I were over, that he didn't even have to be here to win.

The next minute I was alone, both men gone.

Brady left the hotel, Sasha caught the bus for Mexico City.

All day I searched for Brady—the American Legion, the Cuc, Hotel Sautto, casas of friends, the Fragua, La Mamacita, between the swinging doors of his favorite cantinas, as women have done for eons searching for their man. Nobody had seen him. By comida I knew he'd left town.

I went wild, lay on the bed and screamed and cried and moaned, shouted at the walls, at Brady. Lupita, the guest next door, knocked, "Are you ill, Alicia?"

I phoned his sister in Houston, his mother in Moulton, his priest friend and mentor Father Jerome in Chicago, and told them all to have him phone me the moment they heard from him. If they did. None had. Emergency, I said, emotional breakdown, utter misunderstanding, come back at once. "Are you sick?" his sister asked.

I wrote letters to him at each place, explaining that I loved him, couldn't live without him, couldn't bear to lose him, didn't want any other man, that this comparison shopping had been no more interesting than tossing out stuff for the Salvation Army. Come back, my angel darling, the only man I want in my dotage. I mailed all the letters airmail special delivery, slugged tequila in my room, fell asleep weeping.

Next day I dragged out of bed and slumped through the first day of the rest of my life alone, all my own doing through vanity. Yes, vanity! Remember the night at La Mamacita I had to pull a woman's arm off him that he'd made a date with when I told him to get lost? Did I ever deserve it.

That night I dreamt Brady had never left San Miguel, that he was here in town. I saw him with a slick looking *chica* in a Mercedes. Brady saw me and he felt bad, leaving me and living with her, but he'd never been a peacock. At ease for the first time in his life. I'd taught him how to be strong, how to take, demand, enjoy. A middle-aged man is king, sought by rich women, pretty ones but not as pretty as I am but almost. I slashed my wrists, he fell into my bloody arms, did the same. On the night of the Day of the Living Dead we got married in bandages. We quieted down. Day dawned, gray awakening.

A week later Brady phoned. "I climbed Mount Popo then went back to Texas. Do you mean this letter?"

"Come back. Yes. Come back."

Size thirteen pointing east, size thirteen pointing west, darling angel Brady loped to my room, his beard grown bushy and shapeless, waving my letter. He paused in the doorway and read it aloud, fending me off. "Sign that again and date it," said Brady. I did. "Now you may kiss me."

Through the spikes I kissed his soft lips. "Your beard sprouted. It looks vile."

"That's why you love me."

"I don't love you."

Brady patted the letter in his shirt pocket. "Because I'm infinitely correctible. You'll never run out of things to fix." Brady picked me up, one leg on each side of his waist. "How's Love Britches?" and carried me out to the sun terrace.

"Darling pie, did you bring your scissors?"

I, Alicia, sat on his lap on the sun terrace and trimmed his beard. We made a goatee this time. Suddenly his Mistress missed Junie.

"Junie's gone away," said Brady. Then Growling Daddy picked up Darling Daughter and carried her back to the room and pressed her back—lifting her top and lowering her pants—against the cold mirror for mirror torture. Darling daughter, quite naturally, hollered. They fell on the bed and he told her today's story.

"Today Darling Daughter is playing in the warm spring at the foot of the Matterhorn where it's seventy-two degrees and green all year, and you can pick grapes right off the vine, some

mature, some still ripening, and some fermented so they're almost as good as wine."

"You can see the snow from the green?"

"Of course," said Growling Daddy, "this is paradise. And
lots of men are there in the spring."

"Oh, I love it here."

"And they all look like Father Brady."

"Ohhhh," I moaned. "You look gorgeous in the goatee."

"Poor Alicia, poor old girl," laughed Brady. "She's hooked."

"Shut up and kiss me."

Brady surely did.

Idle Hands

I've known three murderers in my life, all in Mexico. One was *gringo*, one was *Mexicano*, and one, Vicente, was half-and-half. Vicente was caught in the ghost town, Pozos, trying to dump the body into one of the many deep abandoned mineshafts—open, anybody could stumble in. Nobody knew or cared to delve five hundred feet down for possibilities every time a murder ran out of town.

Vicente had heard moans from the trunk where he'd stashed the tall skinny old fool. He was dead. That last blow had done it, he'd checked his breathing. Shaking, Vicente slammed the brakes on, opened the trunk, and saw the old nut was gasping, feebly, almost but not quite done in. Vicente strangled the old man to death. He had to get this over with. Then with the full moon's light, he dragged him to the nearest mine shaft.

Cruising Federales saw him profiled on the ridge, arrested him, drove him to Guanajuato to jail. Vicente confessed quickly. He did not wish to be beaten. He did not wish to stay in the harsh serious Guanajuato state prison. He wanted to go home to San Miguel with its friendly men's *cárcel* right on the Jardín, next to the *Presidencia*.

Why had he done it? I, Alicia, intended to find out. Long ago in the deep past, a man had almost strangled me to death.

Vicente loved to talk literature and art, a rare man. He knew pre-Columbian history—Aztecs, Huastecs, Tarascans, Amuzgas, Chichimecas, Otomis, Toltecs, Zapotecs, Lacandon Maya, even how they intertwined with their gods. He spoke Nuahuatl. We were intellectual buddies. Even if I were half-starved for a man, I'd never have made him a boyfriend. He'd been engaged to my dear friend, Azucena, and what she told me would make any woman leery.

Vicente belonged to the social set. His family didn't work. They owned. Houses, land, rental houses and apartments, three large ranches. His family, four hundred years in the New World, fought the Revolution against Spain with Ignacio Allende and Padre Hidalgo, survived the 1910-20 Revolution against their *hacendado* class, reclaimed their status in the *Cristo* rebellion of the 1930s, married foreigners, usually *gringas* and *Europeas* who were incontestably white. Vicente's mother was American. Vicente enlisted in the Navy then went to Amherst then lived in New York. But everybody works so hard in the States that he got bored and came home.

Vicente had never married but then he was only forty. Many *altagente* gents play around till they get tired, then marry a twenty-year-old. Vicente looked like anybody—fairly tall, balding dark hair, strong frame, beginning paunch. Long face, serious dark eyes with Spanish tilt, well curved brows. Everybody liked him.

Eva said, "He did the town a favor, Alicia, by killing that doddering old German pedophile."

Vicente and Ivan lived in the same hilly wooded gated community. At seventy, tall skinny stooped Ivan was cantankerous, nasty to everybody, much disliked. Though he had a longtime British lover of only sixty with a fancy palacio, he preferred Mexican boys of eleven-thirteen. Poor boys who'd do anything for ten pesos, for a meal, a shirt. He liked to hear them scream.

Vicente and Ivan quarreled about the garbage, the loud TV, parking, noisy company. The night of the murder Vicente came home from a party and encountered Ivan outside his house. They fought about the young boys which Ivan considered nobody's business. Louder and louder, more heated. Vicente hit him and old Ivan fell. Vicente kicked him as Ivan struggled. Vicente kicked him almost to death, stomped his chest, kicked his head, beat him till he was done, threw the body into his car and drove out of town toward the silver mineshafts of Pozos.

A Raskolnikov tale but hardly worthy of Dostoyevsky. Was that why he did it? To kill evil.

This semester I was teaching working class kids as well as cops and criminals, ex- inmates, that is. John Jay College of Criminal Justice is part of loony CUNY. Were *they* ever honing my enquiring mind! In my Creative Writing class, the kids wrote about their poor violent families. Cops wrote about shootouts, about almost shooting an undercover guy, about miracle arrests where the felon threw his gun down. In one class I had a parolee and his arresting officer. Ex-inmates wrote about unfair trials, prison, dope deals where dealers turned them—the mules—in. Who told the truth? Writing a police report, concocting a story, develops narrative skill. Almost all the black cops had been spread-eagled and frisked as juveniles, which was *why* they became cops.

Once I asked a class how many had never experienced physical violence. No hands went up. Then I asked how many had experienced physical violence at home. Every hand went up. All the kids said they preferred living with a single parent, their mother.

Since Vicente confessed, he'd have his Hearing before a judge next month. Everyone was horrified when they read his grim confession in *Atención*, the bilingual newspaper. So horrified they refused to visit. Others were so horrified they became regulars. Before long, you needed a private sitting for visiting hours. I was so horrified I wanted to ask *why*. Oddly, I was the only person who ever asked directly.

Once I read his Confession, my suffocation effect came back. Being small, I was as feeble as old Ivan. The man was a radio announcer. He strangled me almost to death because I wouldn't kiss him.

A ver Vicente? asked the guard and waved me to a small square room with a desk and bench. A stout pretty Señora searched my *bolsa* then politely patted me down the sides for concealed weapons. They made me leave my sombrero and waved me to the familiar open rectangular court, with the long concrete bench filled with people lining one side. Above, the pure burning blue sky. At the back was Vicente by himself. There were no guards around, just prisoners and their families and guests. I was the only *gringa* but Vicente was the only semi-*gringo* prisoner.

Vicente leapt forward to greet me, arms out, and we embraced awkwardly. Ambiguities of moral revulsion and old habits of friendship. "You look good," I said. In an old straw hat and thong sandals, light pants and shirt, Vicente looked better than I'd ever seen him. A month in jail and the paunch was gone. His face was no longer shapeless but oval and lean and even handsome, with longish sideburns and good mustache, giving him a Latin elegance. Suspend judgment, I told myself, or you'll learn nothing.

First, a tour of the *cárcel*. "This is Uptown," Vicente led me through a large iron grill door, steel plating the bottom half, into the Dormitory, where there were forty or so cots with ropes strung above where prisoners hung their clothes. They live together. Their bunks were covered with blankets and bright serapes, straw floor mats between. At one end were bookcases and at the other, a giant TV, everything orderly and casual. The twenty-foot high ceiling gave their dorm spaciousness and gloom. Then Vicente walked me through the Drunk Tank. "Downtown," he said. Twelve or so men sat on thin mats on the stone floor. Drunks are thrown in to sleep it off overnight. "Buenas tardes, Señorita," once again, several said courteously.

We entered the soccer court where two serenely overweight Señoras sold chile from huge pottery *casuelas*, as in the market. Above this court was a guard tower and an ancient unused Keep with gun slots. "We play soccer and handball," Vicente, the proud host, showed me around. There were four bathrooms with aquamarine steel doors and in the back, a clothesline. In one corner, a stone cubicle for private talks, meaning conjugal visits.

"A fascinating jail," I said.

Past a small TV room were two shacks the trustees had built themselves for privacy, each a cube six feet high covered in burlap with an entrance door. At the corner of that room was

Solitary, a windowless room with skylights where men are put if they pull a punch, or worse.

"A guy was just in for a week," Vicente said, "for trying to escape."

Trustees are paid and sell refrescos. "Whatever you want, marijuana, of course." One trustee they didn't like but voted back in because his sentence was about to expire. "He knew if he went out he'd be killed," Vicente said, "by the brothers of the woman he did in. He's better off inside."

Vicente pointed, "Over there is the room where they work 'em over. We know because it smells. They worked over four guys to get to Sally the dealer."

"My friend, Vanessa, the assistant DA, visited Sally in the Women's Jail."

Back to the sunny courtyard where the family visits were like a subdued fiesta. Facing the court inmates lounged in front of the three private rooms, which can be rented by those with *moneda* who wish to be alone or with a roommate. Vicente sat on an *equipal* stool and I sat on the long concrete bench beside the *criada* who'd brought food from his mother. I was reluctant to plunge in directly and Vicente obviously needed to talk.

"When I came in, I was pretty wild. I got challenges and taunts from all sides. But I had to learn to get along. We all do. Dormitory living is the way a cárcel should be. You get crazy in cells. Dorm living rehabilitates because you have to live with everybody else close together. There are about forty of us. When somebody starts trouble, we restrain him then we all sort of retrain him, show him the limits, so everybody is usually courteous. They have to be."

Was Vicente showing *me* the limits? Urging me to zip my lip? Sucked into the black hole, I'd entered a parallel universe.

"We have three groups—the Hard Murderers who did it with a pistola, the Soft Killers who did it with a knife—or like me," he reddened but didn't look up, "and the Violins—from *violados*—who are rapists. The Violins are usually very sociable and often implicate a buddy they bring along, and brag about the rape."

What was the best approach? "I'm not interested in *how*, Vicente, but *why*? *Why* did you do it?"

"That's what I ask myself over and over, *why*?" He looked up at me warily. "I had nothing monumental against Ivan but I was crazed." He stared at the ground. "At this big party, they slipped a *substance* into my drink because they wanted me out of the way. Drug transactions were about to happen. I'd told some drug gossip to a guy who'd sold it. The established dealers are protected by the cops—they're all in it together, all the way up."

What a silly cover story, I thought. A Mickey, of all things.

"But I had no idea I could lose control and act so viciously. I knew I was capable of it. But I didn't know I couldn't control myself, when the crime was committed."

When the crime was committed. Not when *I committed* the crime. Ex-inmates in my class talked the same way.

"I've done a lot of figuring and have a lot of forgiving of myself to do. He was a despicable man, impossible to deal with, but that's no excuse."

"*Forgiving yourself?*" I made a sour face. "You may have to deal with uncontrolled viciousness that comes over you, in no relation to a Mickey in a drink," I said with flat disgust.

"Yes, I know. Here I am, I hate to be confined." Vicente handed emptied plates back to the family criada.

"Do the others get food?"

"Everybody gets *atole* and tortillas in the morning, chile at midday, and chile and tortillas at night. But families who can send food."

"You've never had to work, have you?"

"No, and I could never get started on anything," Vicente said. "I called my life Slow Suicide."

At last, I thought. "Write it. Now you have material."

Two PM Unlock. We'd all been locked in for an hour.

"People fear they won't be let out," Vicente smiled. "I'll be out by October, after my Hearing. Money can buy anything here," he buzzed my cheek. "That's how Sally got out."

All the women filed out first and I picked up my sombrero on the bench. The men got out slowly as their names were called. Suppose an inmate tried to walk out with a friend or family name? They'd ask him to duplicate the signature and prevent the other from leaving.

Outside, so unreal it was magic—the Jardín, sunny people, rosy Parroquia, surrounded by greening trees and bird chirp. Astounding blue sky free floating with clouds, no longer a blue rectangle.

"*Hola*, Alicia," several *chicas* from Yoga class.

Older gringas who go blonde with age trolled the Jardín for possibilities. Somber-suited Mexican businessmen gossiped like girls. Surly posing young of every nationality, hanging and sloping like video stars. Ah, freedom.

"Hi, Lies." Lies Wiegman, founder of our *San Miguel Writer* literary mag, sat at a table selling copies. I bought several because my story, "*Quetzalcoatl Returns*" was in the current issue, along with a new poem by Donald Finkel. Lies, retired Dutch photo-journalist, had published her famous photos of Salvador Dali and his wife Gala on the Riviera in our first issue.

Malignant gossip spread like typhus through the town. Vicente was a kleptomaniac. Vicente was a closet queen who serviced older gays.

The day after the crime—this was true—he was to appear before a judge accused of stealing five thousand dollars from Phil, a crazy lawyer, who claimed to have thirty thousand dollars cash he was toting to Guadalajara To Get A Better Exchange Rate. Phil had two guns he waved around and tried to pass to Vicente to hold. Vicente thought Phil's wife took the money because he constantly threatened to kill her. But they'd stayed overnight with Vicente—Holy Week, hotels were full—and Phil accused Vicente who'd said, "When I was in the Navy, if something was missing from a foot locker, the one who let his property disappear was considered stupid."

Alicia's Theory of Gossip: gossip leaps to the most extreme or dramatic act that imaginatively fits the circumstances. But Vicente did have mental problems. He disassociated. In the midst of conversation, he'd be off talking to air, to an invisible person, for two seconds, ten seconds, then come back, as if nothing had happened.

San Miguel had its felons on the run—the matronly caterer who'd fleeced an M.D., Ginny's sublet who held a garage sale and sold all her furniture. As well as remittance loonies like English Anne, and impressive phony movie producers, scriptwriters, generals, bankers, not to mention your standard blocked writer or painter whose work no human eye had ever seen. That grand old bohemian expat gang. English Anne, by the way, had now gone gay and was living with the six-foot tall super rich Mexican lesbian, Lola Lulu. Cliff Irving skipped out, leaving his host a two thousand dollar phone bill.

Every charity in town had its treasury ripped off at least once. Big event, everybody volunteers, town comes and spends. Proceeds disappear. Brady and I got tired of it and got *Atención* to demand charities report their gross and net for the public to see in print.

Phony Mexican architect married young American heiress, so madly in love with him she sank six hundred thousand dollars into retirement homes in the *campo*. He built a one-room concrete office then disappeared. Wanted for scams all over *el país*. The gringo wanted in Boston for bank fraud who ripped off the year's hottest dramatic production. Formed his own investment scheme and gringos and Mexicans who *knew* this invested with him.

At least, Vicente confessed his full evil and is doing jail time.

With the best lawyer in town paid twenty thousand dollars by his family, Vicente did *not* skip away after his Hearing. The judge convicted Vicente of premeditated murder and sentenced him to twenty years, reduced to twelve, which means he might be out in six years, as three-fifths of a year counts as a year.

The following summer, Vicente greeted me with a big embrace in the courtyard of our local cárcel. He'd been in a year.

"Oh, the food's here," says Vicente and we go to the open interior court where two women serve lined-up prisoners *arroz picante con roja papas*. This special treat is donated daily by a sympathetic storekeeper in the market. When we pass the conjugal cubicle, Vicente says, "They say I'm queer because I don't have conjugal visitors. But it would only make me hornier if I started. I'm better off this way. It really is a monastery, you know. I like that." Off a dark doorway I saw an elaborate altar, *Nuestra Seño-ra*, with ribbons and glittery paper, blue flowers and lit candles.

"First, the news," I said. Vicente liked to hear what he was missing. "The literary readings Marty Cramer started have gone bigtime, moved to Bellas Artes. Marty and Bix still have the big blowout after." Marty, serious doper, taught Painting at Instituto Allende. Bix, his German wife, said to me, "Why haven't you slept with Marty? Everybody else has."

Vicente hooted.

"And you know Clarence, the blocked black painter? Well, Terry Burke, the dike parolee and poet, got a letch for his white teenage wife. The two held a knife fight around Clarence's kitchen table. Terry was winning, Clarence jumped out the window."

Vicente sighed. "I *am* better off in here."

Vicente introduces me to two sexy-looking young women with a handsome guy in cowboy duds. Both women shake my hand, giving the *compadre* hands up slap at the end. In the visitors' courtyard Vicente says those are the man's two sisters and that he and another man killed a taxi driver.

"They were stoned on grass—the family is a bad bunch of gypsies growing marijuana over by Guanajuato—and they were fooling around with a gun in the backseat and the driver told them to cool it and the gun went off. The mother tried to sell marijuana in Guanajuato and they jailed *her* over there. They're awful thieves."

I jumped in. "Vicente, I heard you were at a Scrabble party with various middle-aged couples. No drugs involved. You're evading *why.*"

Vicente stared at me, past me. "I'm part Latino, you know," he began, "I respond to *words* and Ivan was vicious, he called me things and accused me of things. When I was a boy, I played hand-ball, every day from age twelve to twenty, and my hands are the first things that react." Vicente held his idle hands out, fingertips touching, inspecting them for the answer. They're not big hands.

"I've had this violence in me since I was a boy. I've felt it but I'd always repressed it, well, lots of my feelings. I'd decided I wasn't going to work, compete, I wasn't going to marry. I thought only of myself. Several women wanted to marry me, but no. You can't live that way. It does something awful to you inside. The few weeks before, I felt something build up in me and get stronger and stronger and I knew that soon my life was going to change completely, I didn't know how, but I knew it was coming."

That hair-trigger violence in men. In Las Vegas, after graduate school, after my young husband left me for another woman, I was there for a divorce. I wrote copy for NBC and he was a CBS announcer I met at a station party. A middleclass man tried to strangle me to death. A middleclass man with, it turned out, a family.

I reached into my pocket. "My money is gone!"

"Oh, God, I hope they didn't pick your pocket."

"Maybe I dropped it."

"Everything dropped gets picked up and you never see it again."

We go to look and in the dormitory, the cowboy gypsy holds out the paper clipped money and says, "Is this yours?"

"Gracias, muchísimas gracias," I gush.

Vicente gives him a friendly arm. "I'll never forget your kindness," Vicente says, moved. We stroll back to the courtyard. "I've been working on him, I talked to him about Christian charity, not just taking everything. I'm impressed."

"So am I."

"You see, because he met you, because he was introduced, he was a gentleman." We settle, sun in my face on the court-length stone bench. I, Alicia, the only middleclass visitor among the poor families.

"I know you *hit* Azucena," I said. His former *novia*, Azucena, told me she was asleep and he *socked* her across the face, yelling slut and whore and screaming at her. They went to a therapist. Nothing was resolved. He hit her again, harder. She broke their engagement.

"Only with an open hand. Never a closed fist, because I was told that does real damage to a woman."

"*Only?*" Scapegoating again. "Now I know *why* you did it," I said. "Because you *wanted* to. Because you *could*."

Vicente's face seemed to fall away from itself. He got up and walked away, swiped his hands down alongside his face, then sighed slowly as he sat down again.

"It was the only time in my life I felt completely in control. He feared me, he begged me, he fought back with puny strength, making me punch harder to win, to smash his arrogance." He breathed hard, spoke low. "Only a murderer understands—we initiates." He searched my face. "I don't tell other people these things."

"I know."

My puny strength, like Ivan's. His steel hands squeezed my neck. He stretched his body away from me so I couldn't touch him. He pushed my head under the steering wheel. I struggled till my head was up and he stuffed my head into the passenger seat. I couldn't breathe, I knew I was about to die. I kicked wildly, ferociously, and the hard toes of my high heels broke his windshield.

That broke his spell.

The MD pulled glass out of my legs and said I'd have a horrifying sore throat.

My boss begged me not to go to the cops. A blurry little woman, his wife, begged me, "We have three mouths to feed. He'll lose his job." My divorce lawyer got $300 from the man.

Slow suicides often want to take someone along. "You wasted two whole lives," I sobbed, for myself as well. I almost died at twenty-one.

Enraged at himself, he scapegoated the world. It was all so obvious, the reason. "My grandmother said, if you don't *use* a *good* brain, it rots."

Vicente changed the subject. "Want a *refresco*, Alicia?"

"Sure. Mango."

He came back with my Boing mango and his coke.

"I'm teaching English. Never felt so useful," he suddenly grinned. "I'm happy as a clam, I'm helping other prisoners, counseling. I'm the Old Man, they come to me for advice."

"The jailhouse lawyer?"

"One guy had been in fifteen years on trumped up charges, so I wrote the Governor—looked up a little law—and he's out, free. The men trust me. I'm happy—without pressure for the first time in my life. I have books, I'm studying. I met the Governor. I wrote such articulate letters, he offered me a job in his office."

I doubted that but I smiled. I couldn't help liking Vicente.

"For the first time in my life, I'm useful. The other day I looked up at our blue rectangle of sky," his eyes went moist, he pulled his hat down, "and I felt the rapture of being alive."

My suffocation effect: I wake up unable to breathe with my head stuck under a blanket so heavy I can't lift it because my arms can't move. Abruptly I gasp and breathe, head out of the covers. Slowly, in the dreaming night, my suffocation effect swirls to sleep again. That small death would always be part of my body, to resurrect at will. I didn't call it a trauma because I hoped to minimalize it. But when I first moved to New York, every night I felt a man move under my bed.

When he got out five years later, Vicente was older, quieter, more scholarly. He meant to go back in and keep helping the guys. But he couldn't make himself go back inside. People pointed at him on the streets and whispered. Others, like me, ducked and finally gave him a hug and chatted.

After several weeks Vicente began looking hopeless again. "Alicia," he said, "I miss my *compadres.*"

Vicente went to the *Bodega de Sorpresas* and bought some jeans and sweaters then to the *Mercado de Martes* and bought a bunch of T-shirts. At the jail they inspected his gifts cautiously. Vicente and I hauled the load to the dormitory and he hollered, "*Feliz Cumpleaños por todos.*"

"*Hola, compadre, que tal, cuantas chicas has chingada?*" High fives from the guys, shoves like hugs, solemn handshakes.

"Anybody need a letter written? Messages?" Vicente wrote birthday greetings to Mama from her devoted son, Juan Carlos. Then the gypsy brother and one of his sisters approached, he in cowboy duds as ever and she actually wearing an off-the-shoulder gypsy peasant blouse, bright red.

Rojena, the sister, dictated a distracted note to her mother in jail in Guanajuato: "Mama, we miss you, we need you to plan. Ricardo and I tell you, Mama, to stop fighting the other women or they will never let you out. Be good, Mama, so we see you before too long. *Tu hija*, Rojena."

As she licked the envelope, Rojena looked long at Vicente.

"*Vamos por un cafecito*," suggested Vicente.

"*Ándele,*" Ricardo grinned.

Rojena made Vicente feel like Rip Van Winkle waking up after forty-six years on planet Earth.

Yes, Rojena admitted, "*Soy una ladrona, una ratera*, a thief, I cheat and lie, I have stabbed two men."

"*Me alegre.*" This made Vicente happy.

Rojena was certainly not of his own class and he liked that. His own class had ceased to interest him. His own class was asleep, he realized, in the midst of a torrent. A torrent of multitudes that one day would pour down from the *guerilla* hills, already living in these very mountains, they say. Here, not just in Chiapas.

Before long Vicente decided he had to tame her and they married. Now and then Rojena disappears for a couple of days, a roving beast. Vicente accepts that. He has to, if he wants to keep her. Everybody wanted to meet them. Their tale tantalized newcomers. They became local celebrities. Just like home.

Wanted and Unwanted

First, you have to get the lice out of their hair.

Guy bathed the girls when they arrived with their twenty-three-year-old mother. Every time they came, Guy said, he had to pick and scrub to get the lice out of their itchy hair. Hair that looked dead as an old burro.

Rosalba, the mother, swayed her hips as she strolled to the hotel terrace, followed by her four tiny girls. The eldest, age eight, huffed as she carried the baby girl. The Otomi mother and little girls looked out of place on the terrace of the red tile-roofed hotel, with its arched columns and flowing plants in great earthen pots. Guy and I both had rooms on the second floor, facing the long rose washed terrace, where I read research in the afternoon, gazing at distant blue Sierras.

In the morning I write in my room, while the bluest sky I've ever seen flies huge white cumulus over the town. Under hundred-year-old trees, I walk through the lush green Mexican hotel garden, profuse with lilies and fig and banana trees, bordered by *huele de noche*, the bell shaped rosy blooms that openly offer perfume only at night.

While the young mother bathed in Guy's room, Mary Grace cooked the food in her apartment at the end of the terrace. Then

Guy set out a big round glass table with chairs for everybody to sit and eat. A merry family group. Sustained by Guy the gringo, Guy the late middle-aged blue-eyed junior high math teacher. Never a milder man, almost the epitome of bland. Brown gray hair, average height, average build, slightly more boring than average. His soft swooning blue eyes were wasted on his wan personality. Guy was never lively, always calm as stone.

When Rosalba the mother swished out to the terrace, she looked sexy and gaudy elegant. A bright petal blossomed among poorest weeds. Already she had four little girls, Graciela age eight, Flor age five, Dopey age three, and a baby girl, Crucita.

Mary Grace was the mother of my friend Vanessa, assistant DA in San Antonio. When her husband left her for his secretary, Mary Grace retired from marriage and the US. She served a rich pork stew—Guy did the buying—and Guy bought cokes for everybody. I watched their joy, marveling at the goodness of certain expats. Mary Grace ducked back into her place and emerged with handmade dresses for each girl, that she'd sewn on her own machine. Like most San Miguel Norteamericanas, she'd turned blonde with age and rounded out. Mary Grace sewed like a French seamstress.

The little girls were awed by rich food, nice dresses. Probably they had meat once a year, at Christmas. They ate gingerly then hungrily while all the adults smiled upon the wondrous scene. Then Mary Grace scooped up the baby and took the little girls to her apartment to try on their new dresses. Guy escorted their mother, Rosalba, into his room. It was so quiet you knew something was up.

What a kind fellow is Guy, I thought, to help out this entire poor family because he sleeps with the mother, and gives her money. He actually seems interested in the four little girls.

Then Rosalba and the girls piled into Guy's car and he returned them to the flimsy cardboard and tin hovel in the canyon where they lived. On the hillside above, great trucks and buses roared day and night, circling the rising *Carocol* that skirted town, leading up to the high plateau blacktop to Querétaro. The tin shook, the tarred cardboard wavered and had to be propped up again. Every piece of scrap metal was Found Wall, for reinforcement. Rosalba and her four daughters shared the one-room shack with her parents, two brothers and one sister. Ten in one room. They squatted, poorest of the poor.

When Guy's car parked in front, it was longer than the house.

"Guy interviewed eight young women," Mary Grace explained it to me. "He'd asked Serena, our upstairs maid, to send them to him for 'work'. Rosalba was the only one who toted her kids along."

"He chose the most needy," I said, "the one with the children."

"Heartbreaking, those tiny girls," said soul-of-a-nun Mary Grace. "Filthy as pigs, Alicia, first time they came."

Moist eyed, we hugged. Goodness, it slays me.

"We feed them three times a week. Now I'm shopping for sweaters." Mary Grace sighed, "Guy bought beds for the shack. They slept on pallets, Alicia, on the ground."

"Vanessa phoned *me*," I said. "She's so happy with Jake. Brooks is six now. She's running for District Attorney—*que cojones!*"

"Yes! I do *wish* Vanessa could bring Jake back to the Church," Mary Grace sighed.

"Vanessa?" I laughed. "Fat chance." On the way to comida, I passed Guy. "What you two are doing is wonderful," I said.

"I had all boys," Guy said with his sweet bland smile. "Girls are a novelty, a change."

Serena, our upstairs maid, disapproved. "She's always *muy elegante* and *las niñas* very dirty. Soap costs less than *pintura*," Serena scolded. "But Rosalba spends the money he gives her on lipstick and new blouses."

With her Spanish features and Indian skin, her long black glossy hair, Serena, at twenty-eight, was the youngest and prettiest maid. Serena and I exchanged gossip as I'd known her for years. When I left for New York in the fall, I always tipped her well. All the hotel employees were paid minimum wage, no matter how many years they'd worked.

Serena supported her four children working six days a week. When her husband, an unemployed construction peon, became an abusive *borracho*, Serena and her brood went home to her father's one-room concrete rental shack.

"Rosalba is *floja*, doesn't like to work," Serena flicked the wet mop to and fro on my ceramic tile floor, as close to anger as I'd ever seen her. "She lives in a mud hovel. She takes Señor Guy's money, says it's for *las niñas* and pays off with sex."

"Speaking of sex," I said, "have you met anybody interesting this summer?"

"Rosalba confided in me," Serena was not to be swayed from the liaison. "She told me *no tiene felicidad*, she finds no joy, with Guy, el viejo, that she just does it for the money. I don't respect her, Alicia." Serena wafted the feather duster vaguely toward my windows. "A woman has to be able to touch with pleasure the man."

"I agree completely." Years ago when they were first married, Serena told me how much she loved to sleep like spoons with her new husband, how good he smelled, how gentle he was with their first two infants.

"*Hay más*," said Serena. "Remedios says one of Rosalba's girls is from Remedios' own husband." Remedios was the oldest maid, who worked in the front section of the hotel. "She doesn't like that a bit, Alicia, especially since this child of her husband is the best of the lot, Remedios says."

"You know which one?" I asked.

Serena shook her head, in disgust.

Rosalba and her girls were our guests on the terrace three days a week. Before long, I was chatting with all of them. The children now had tiny bathrobes and sandals. Rosalba brought their dirty clothes in a laundry bag Guy supplied and he took them to the laundromat. Mary Grace sized the four girls' shoulders so she could buy winter jackets for all. Vixen-eyed Rosalba tossed her long cascade of black curls, crossed her slim ankles, in her new high heels and slithery rayon dress, and posed for the curious.

When Brady and I came back to San Miguel the next summer, I bumped into Guy and three of the little girls at the high red metal gate of their garden enclave of houses near Parque Juárez. All over town these twelve-foot high locked guard gates have convenient little strings anyone can pull to open the locks. We buzzed cheeks.

"The girls have grown," I noticed.

"I'm big now," said Flor, at six.

"You said that in English," I said.

"Guy taught us English," said nine-year-old Graciela, as easily as any child from the States.

"Come see the house," said Guy with his bland pleased smile.

Guy and the three girls lived in a house near ours with seven rooms, two baths, various small TVs, children's dolls and toys everywhere. Guy now had a concert piano to practice on, Mozart on the stand. "By now, they're here full time," said Guy. "They go home on weekends to see their grandparents, and the baby."

"Where's Rosalba?"

Guy almost blushed. "She's living with her new novio, a young man, and she's *embarazada* again."

"Pregnant, with her fifth, at twenty-four?" Mexico was drenched, drowning, choked in fertility. Among the poorest, eight children was average. Blame machismo, blame Catholicism, blame poverty. Blame the rich. The Sunday evening *paseo* in the *Jardín* was now a crowd jam, not a stroll.

"Yes, but she visits," said Guy. "Flor, get ready for your piano lesson. And Graciela, put on shoes you can dance in. Classes," Guy sighed.

Pretending they're not watching, these old babes. Old babes with laser beam eyes and falling flesh. While I dip into soft tender fragrant buds, delicate as pistils and quivering with awakening. Desire—a new world for them, opened with infinite care and patient regard by their dear dad.

My aim was simple—never to look at anything less than beautiful. Connoisseur of sublimity in its budding. Since I myself could NOT be sublime, I became eyes, hands, fresh inhalation, touch oh touch. The first time I bathed that flesh, I knew it was mine. Smooth filthy dark brown turning flower sweet beige brown with our bath.

Listening to the three chatter in English, I said, "Guy, you've accomplished a miracle."

Little girls who'd ordinarily drop out of school at sixth grade, unable to read or write Spanish, now learned English, as well. The meal ticket language. Guy was educating them in a good bilingual school. They almost looked like schoolchildren. But they were smaller and thinner due to poverty.

"In the house we speak only English," said Guy.

"And do homework," moaned Flor, the squashed-face little charmer, ugly and smart. Bold Flor. Graciela at nine was already a sixteen-year-old beauty with regular serene features, but she was far from smart. Both girls now had great mops of shiny silky black hair. Shy Graciela. Dopey at four was always a mess, rolling in the sand pile or falling off the log set up beside the house for the girls to walk on. Dopey grinned but I couldn't get a word out of her in any language. The girls played hide-and-seek in the mini-crop of corn Guy grew in their back patio.

"Guy, I couldn't be more impressed," I said.

Once Rosalba moved out of Guy's house with her young novio, people whispered that Guy was a pedophile. Unusual charity is hard to comprehend.

That's what we all want—flower beauty, pure scent—and I'm the one with the courage to do it. Because I LOVE them, as well. They're my beloved family, my darling daughters. THEY love me. Did my boys? They hated me. They had eyes only for Margaret. For Mama.

The old women are jealous, I know. Always inviting me to parties. They want my flesh but theirs makes me puke. They think I'm SIN-NING. Ho, ho. Wouldn't they fall over if they discovered I was giving BIRTH?

When Brady arrived from New York, we had moved into a house in the same quiet garden enclave near Guy and the girls. Gonging and chiming, church bells woke us at dawn. We loved them. A young nun swung playfully on the bell rope. Little girl laughter like tinkling bells rang through the grounds. Mary Grace visited us when she dropped off delicacies or darling tams or sox with lace frills for the girls. Grinning with pride, she whipped out a snapshot taken with Vanessa, her daughter.

"She's gorgeous as ever," I said. "Did she win the election?"

"Now she's a big shot," said Mary Grace. "DA in Baer County, San Antonio."

Before we left in the fall, we gave Guy money to buy boots for the girls.

"Flor, you're getting prettier," I greeted her the next summer. Her face had shifted planes from ugly to cute. At ten Graciela's small breasts bloomed to suit her mature beauty face. Dopey had actually mastered some English and talked almost normally.

"I'm here in Mexico to stay," Guy told me. "I have no desire to even see the U.S. again."

"Why not?

"Why?" said Guy, in his rocker on the porch with Dopey and Crucita, the tiny toddling girl, climbing on him. "It doesn't get any better than this."

Covering myself with nubile children crawling all over me like baby kittens. Touching, tuning, turning children into women. Shaman Guy—not shame on Guy. Transforming—one of the few special beings alive who is privileged to see transformation. Transubstantiation.

Transcendence ACTUALLY TAKING PLACE – DOING IT. Not before or after but unfolding nooowwwww. Fancy thoughts, these, but my own.

Here she comes, my neighbor, Ms. Doubter. My two littlest tumbling, winding around me like eels.

I put my arms behind my head, sighed. "Did I say, it doesn't get any better than this?" I smile paternally at Ms. Curiosity.

She grins happily. I've satisfied her. Her own inadmissible LUST. Ho, I see it all. In all of them.

Mary Grace, now more white than blonde and more round than not, hugged me hello the next summer. After comida I stopped by her apartment for a drink, to find out about Guy's strange request.

"Guy knows my daughter is a DA," said Mary Grace. "He asked me to check if he was free to visit the US or was there still a warrant out for him."

"A warrant for his arrest?" *Chi-huahua!*

"Something minor, Faye," shrugged Mary Grace. "Vanessa can check national police records."

By now all four girls lived with Guy. Rosalba and her new novio had the care only of their new baby girl. Rosalba would drop off the new baby and go about her business. The baby, Milagros, wailed and screeched when Rosalba left her there overnight. The little girls vied for turns carrying the lusty baby, Milagros.

Pale and trembling, Mary Grace grabbed my arm. "Come," she led me to her apartment. "Vanessa checked police records. Guy is wanted in Santa Cruz for child sexual abuse.

Two fourteen-year-old girls, his junior high students, filed suit against Guy for rape, sexual assault. There's a warrant out for his arrest."

"Oh God!" I groaned.

Guy had jumped bail, that first summer at the hotel, and fled to Mexico, to San Miguel, hideout of the unwanted and the Wanted. Mostly dope dealers and fraud.

"He picked the *only* young woman who came with children," Mary Grace was stricken. "I should've known."

"What shall we do?" I wanted to grab the four girls and run. "Tell him he can't go back? Tell him we know?"

"I can't face him, Alicia," Mary Grace's eyes watered. "I'm too appalled."

"Maybe he asked you, Mary Grace, because he wants *help*," I said. "He wants to put you and himself on notice *not* to repeat the act. Why else would he have asked you to find out? Since he already knew what the answer would reveal?"

We both felt queasy. "Why don't we talk to Rosalba the mother?"

Several days later, as Rosalba strutted to Guy's house, I ran to get Mary Grace. As she left through the vine arbor walkway, we confronted her.

"Rosalba, hello," I said. "We were wondering if there's space with you and your new novio for the four girls?"

"Why?" she glared at me.

"You're their mother," said Mary Grace in her sweet sentimental tone.

"They'll be *safer* with you," I laid it out. "Guy is a *man*, after all."

"There's no space," Rosalba's look of sulky suspicion made me feel I was beating her with a stick. "I don't want the girls back. I can't care for them." Now she shrieked, "Besides, they are my father's responsibility. Two of them. They are *his children*."

"But, but I thought they were *your* children," Mary Grace said.

"They are," Rosalba ducked her head. "*By him.*"

"Put Guy on notice you're watching," I said to Mary Grace.

"I can't do it, Alicia, I can't face him." One day she said she'd told Guy her daughter-in-law had not been able to find out anything.

Neither of us thought Guy had done it *yet*. All four girls were clean, healthy, educatable, smiling. Their black hair shone, they played and chattered like little girls. At the family shack, they had two uncles and their grandfather, who was really their father. Here in the nice big house, there was only Guy. Here in the nice roomy house that now had a tree swing, sandbox, patio walls with steps to walk to the roof, there was only Guy.

In the dead of night in our bed, Brady beside me, I'd sometimes listen. I'd hear a cat scream. Thin piercing shriek. A mumble, did I hear a moan? I watched the girls closely for signs. Everybody watched the girls for signs, even those who didn't know what Mary Grace had discovered. Why did we think there would be any?

First, you have to get the lice out of their hair.

Summers passed and Guy and the girls—now he had adopted all five—were accepted as family. Rosalba now had another new novio and she visited her daughters seldom. "He's going to take me to the States," Rosalba told me proudly. "He'll go first, and arrange for me."

The local young dream was to wetback and work in the States. In poor families I knew, the girls were married and burdened with children and their brothers had all fled to the US to work. Most sent money home. Some married and stayed. Most returned every six months to a year to their Mexican families and got their wives pregnant with the next baby. Saving diligently, they bought a small piece of land and, brick by brick, started to build their *casita*. After oil and tourism, money sent home from the States was Mexico's third largest source of income.

With great amusement Guy told me the story of Flor's first menstruation. "I was so stupid I didn't know what was happening. So I took her to the *Unión Médica*."

"Didn't Graciela explain it to her?"

"Apparently not," smiled Guy.

How did I know my poor child was sick? When she refused to come to my bed, I confess I got angry. Dad, I can't, she moaned and groaned, and when I lifted my hand, she clutched her stomach. I hurt, Dad, so bad, she said.

Next day the médico said, Your little daughter has become a woman. When I seemed confused, he said, She's having her first menses.

No more little girl. I felt deflated, depressed, defeated. If I could turn back the years from twelve to six, the first time my dear one came to me. For three years, I'd stroked, preparing her for my entrance. She was used to half dozing on the bed as I stroked her mound so gently while I read her stories. Subtly, oh so subtly, I flickered my fingers on those sweet plumb lips. Then a dry kiss on each lip before bed in her own private bedroom.

"Come on, girls. Into the car," said Guy. "Want to go to Taboada with us?"

"No, thanks. We went yesterday. Brady is a great swimmer." Taboada was the palm-shaded hot spring swimming pool,

Olympic-size, out in the *campo* with a playground and riding horses. We were neighborly. We sometimes borrowed a sweater or a blanket from Guy.

That summer Flor was surly with her new menses. She stood atop a stonewall enclosure at the high entrance gate and mooned after a boy who worked in an *artesania* outside. *Artesanias* turned the walkway into a souk, selling Huichol beaded figures and snakes and bells, Tarascan masks, black Oaxaca pottery, painted bowls and jewelry and bark primitives. They were made by bright-bloused Indians at the tables, cloth sails on poles to block the sun, their babies playing underneath.

"Flor has a crush on the boy," said Guy pleasantly. "She's getting to that age."

When boys in groups of four or five snuck in to see Flor and Graciela, what could be more normal? Then Guy caught boys on the roof, leaping down onto a dark inner patio to gaze through barred windows at the young girls undressing inside. It happened to me, too, and frightened me, as a girl in the Maryland suburbs. I heard his nails and shoes scrape as he lost his hold on the bathroom window.

One night delicately I tickled her with my hair and stuck my tongue ever so slightly into her tight lip closure. Dad, she squirmed, that feels funny. But it feels good, I told her. The next week—oh, exciting—I enmeshed my tongue between those naked flower petal lips and buttered her baby clitoris. Once a week for six months when she was eight. At nine she moved slightly and said it tickled pretty good.

My drumming fingers played a tattoo she giggled at. Then fingertip touched clit. Surprise! I said, I'm making it grow. What grow? she frowned. Feel and see, I instructed her hand. What's that bump? She was alarmed. I kissed her sweet mouth, inhaling the freshest scent on earth. Then rubbed her till she vibrated. I feel like a train, Dad, she said. Before long, we'll ride it, I explained. Dad, you're loco, she laughed.

Then last summer Guy said Flor was living with her grandmother.

"What about school?" I asked alarmed.

Calmly, Guy said, "I think she'll come back then."

"Don't you miss her?"

"She's here half the time," said Guy. "You know how girls like slumber parties." Guy had a habit of saying reassuringly innocent things to me. Sometimes he seemed to watch too closely for my response.

"Oh, well," I shrugged.

Guy had a complete tool shed. He lent Brady his rake.

"How's Rosalba doing in San Antonio?" I asked.

"A sad story," Guy sighed confidentially. "Her novio says she never arrived, she never got there. Her mother and brother have phoned from here various times. The last time he felt accused and hung up on them." Guy's blue eyes swam. "She's probably dead."

"She wouldn't be the first from here never to make it," I said. "Rosalba had spunk." Poor woman, any horror imaginable probably happened to her.

That would be the second death I'd heard about this week. English Anne, who was always out of control, ran away from Lola, got dead drunk, fell and hit her head the wrong way on jagged cobblestones and died. Age forty-one.

How I worked, slaved, to do my child right. At last when she was nine and ripe to my fragrance needs, my exacting nose, child eyes sparkling as raindrops, her supple little round nubile form, woman in child, I inserted the head of my organ.

For years she'd played it like a toy. I'd told her it was Dad's special toy just for her. That she could make it go from tiny to huge, which she did, laughing. Dad, look how big I got it. Finally I'd said, It's your lolly-pop. Taste just the tip. She did. Dad, I don't like it. Next time I put honey. She licked it off. Dad, that's good. Next time chocolate syrup. She got inventive. We tried whipped cream, canela, guava jelly, guayabana jam. I want the caramel man, she'd say, and I'd dip it in canela. I want the chocolate cone. But my darling always preferred our first choice — honey.

It was Guy's eighth year in San Miguel. Smiling and perkier than usual, Guy went home to Santa Cruz for a three-week visit. Neighbors and a sleep-in maid took charge of the five girls. Guy came back refreshed.

"Good roads, great motels, everything clean," Guy enthused. "I met my grandchildren."

The seven-year Statute of Limitations had expired.

So the first time I entered an inch with a honey tip. We licked honey off each other. Inch by tugging inch till I hit her hymen and she screamed. As my angel cried, I wiped her tears and the blood away. I'm sick, Dad, she said, so I put her to bed.

Don't think I plunged on. I held back behind her hymen for months, then finally touched it. She didn't holler. She was silent. A week later I dipped — not plunged — past her hymen another inch, then once a week another inch. Perhaps three-four in all as she was a child. Then one day my darling moved barely. That feels good, angel. Dad loves you so much. Never more than once a week, as I was wary of overburdening, frightening her off.

Sometimes Flor didn't appear for a week. Then she'd be there at Guy's every day, playing like a child with Dopey and quiet Crucita and athletic Milagros, helping her small sisters. Then surly with adolescence, she'd wander the grounds. Twice she asked me for money to go to Taboada.

"Get it from Guy," I said.

"Dad's not home," said Flor.

"Sorry," I walked off. If he wanted her to go swimming, he'd take her in the car.

The older pretty one, Graciela, visited often, looking like a siren at fifteen. She was living with an aunt.

To make our plane to New York, we had to take the six AM Primera Plus bus. Every fall Guy got up at five AM and drove us to the station. "When I get to the Pearly Gates, I'll be able to say I helped five little girls get a start in life," Guy smiled.

Finally—it had taken years—three?—she accepted my steaming organ and I detected enjoyment. An almost smile.

You're Dad's sweetheart, I told her. You alone of all the girls. How could I confess her older sister to my girl child? My previous practice project which worked out nicely. Except she was getting too old for me at fifteen, a maturely formed female with those unsightly big breasts and hip curves. But she still came to me with her needs, reeking of adolescence—full bloom, not bud. That rotten smell, I hold my breath. Putrefying fish, exactly. In spring the bud poking from the ground is more exquisite by far than the blossom fully extended, spread out and asking for it. Ah, shy bud is my paradise.

Dad, what is that cream that comes out? she asked. It's Dad's milk. Sometimes it makes babies, I said. You make babies, like Mommy? Yes, my little love.

Several months later Mary Grace phoned from Mexico. Guy was out of the house, she told our answering machine; did Brady and I want to rent it?

Oh good, Guy's bought a house, I thought, so he can leave something tangible to the girls. They could always live there as a family, married or divorced, working or with kids. Or as single mothers, a fancy term the millions of them in Mexico wouldn't understand, it's so common.

But the house was a rabbit warren. It didn't appeal to me. I phoned Mary Grace to tell her thanks but no.

"Did Guy buy?" I asked.

"Guy fled for the border, Alicia." Mary Grace explained it to me. "Guy's out of the house."

"What?" I lurched inside.

"Alicia, in the dead of night Guy went to Ruiz Galvan and told him he was sleeping with Flor and Graciela," Mary Grace's voice shook. Ruiz Galvan was the lawyer who lived down the block. "Flor got jealous when she found out about Graciela. She told her grandmother who called the police. Also he took photos of the younger girls nude in the shower. How much to fix it? Ten thousand dollars, cash, Ruiz Galvan told him. Guy couldn't do it. Ruiz Galvan raced him to the bus station and Guy fled for the border. Two hours later the police arrived."

The four girls were back home in the shack.

"Now the police are checking all the Americans who've adopted Mexican children." Mary Grace wept. "It's awful, Alicia."

Any society that treats women as children will treat children as women, said writer Grace Paley. North of the border, as well.

What could I have done? Said? You better watch it. You better not. How would I have known? Even if I'd asked Flor and Graciela if they were having sex, would they know to call it that? If I'd used my hands to make fucky-fucky, would they have understood, told the truth, these offspring of their mother and their own grandfather? They must be crafty enough not to tell the truth to foreign adults. Maybe both girls even thought it was normal. How could they know otherwise? But both, apparently, expected Guy to be faithful. He was the only Dad they ever had.

"When I reach the Pearly Gates," I remember Guy saying one day, looking at us with his mellow swimming blue eyes, "I'll be able to say, I helped five little girls get a start in life."

We Americans felt horrified, guilty. Couldn't we have done *some*thing? But none of us, note, went to the shack to rescue the girls. Maybe next summer I'll see Flor rounding the *Jardín*, sidling up to *gringos*, now that she speaks English. I pray someone will love her.

Maybe it takes a saint or a pedophile to take on the utterly unwanted.

First, you have to wash the lice out of their hair.

The story does not end there. Next summer I bumped into Dopey going to lawyer Ruiz Galvan to get the Money Order Guy sent to her, the ten-year-old he'd not yet possessed. At ten, Dopey was beautiful, well spoken, and now called, at last, Luminada. Guy wrote her and Ruiz Galvan how he missed his family, how lonely he was without them, how specially he loved her, Luminada. It was all, he wrote, Flor's fault.

As the household was broken up when she was nine, he now panted after Luminada, Ruiz Galvan told us. He said Guy told him he initiated each girl at nine. NINE! A puff adder into a kitten. Impaling a child on a spear. Like shoving a baseball bat up a retarded girl, as boys did in New Jersey. Another form of male torture. Like loving to kill, cause damage. These children had been plucked out of the poor for special treatment and special—no, ordinary—torture. Expected violation.

But then, the girls had seemed—happy.

By now Flor was living with Mary Grace and Graciela was still with her aunt, as both girls feared their uncles if they went back home. They were "damaged goods." Flor was back in school.

The following summer Guy was living in Vera Cruz in a far grander house and Grandmother had sent all the girls to him, except Flor. He refused to take Flor the culprit.

A young couple with baby waved furiously. Flor ran toward me, wearing that triumphant smile of young girls who've captured their mate, who smiles with the same boyish pride. It was the boy who worked in the *artesania* outside the gate. They presented their baby. How could the story end there? They were both sixteen.

First, you have to get the lice out of their hair.

Nuestra Señora De La Salud

*B*rady said I had to make him an honest man. I, Alicia, had now permitted Brady to live with me for five years. We're living in sin, said Brady.

This is sin?

It's time we got hitched.

Why?

So I can get right with God.

Brady the tax accountant, ex-Seminarian, ex-monk, is an avid Texas Catholic. There *are* ex-Catholics. There are *no* ex-Texans. I, Alicia, am still teaching at John Jay, where I'm now a full professor, of loonies. Close by is the CPA firm where Brady accounts, that accounts for Brady. I, Alicia, am still a frothy lacy sexnut and Brady is still interested in two things—sex and theology.

God loves you, Brady, I promise.

Ms. Caustic, I can't go to Confession. Five years now.

What do you have to confess, baby? I slung my arms around him. Tell Alicia your dire sins, hmm?

Brady slung off my arms and strode away dramatically.

When I met him those moons ago in San Miguel, Brady was pulling his hair, what was left of it, and moaning, I'm having my

Midlife Crisis, to everyone in earshot. What he meant was, I'm forty and coming out of adolescence. Brady no longer looks like a monk, a timid accountant. Brady now looks like a handsome bearded dude astride Westerns. He has a sweeping quasi-cowboy hat that makes him seem dash itself, smooth and daunting. Woo! Now that he's loved, Brady has the nerve to look good.

When we met, Brady was one of those perfectly good men who lack the power to get women. You'd think they'd learn from observation, from experience. They don't because they lack confidence, a barrier they can't manage to surmount. They're so greatly in need, so starved for sexual continuance, that they have all the power of a bud waiting for rain. But when opened by the possibility of love, they bloom and flower into flamboyant complexity. Smarter, witty, handsome even. At last, because he's loved, Brady has the courage to be handsome. Once I convinced him he was not a sow's ear but a silk purse.

Mother fell for Brady. She wrote me, Your knight on a white horse has arrived. The only man of mine she's tolerated. When he drove us to Arlington Cemetery to visit her father's grave, Brady screamed at me when I told him he'd made a wrong turn. Shrieked like a banshee. Mother whispered, He has no emotional control. I know, I replied, but I think he's harmless. I hope so, she said. So far, I was right. At first, when we came down from New York, she made us stay in a motel because we weren't married. But now that he courted her, astride the white stallion, we stayed in the guest room at home. Did that snake ever know how to play Mother! She's a Southern Lady, he said. A *grand* lady. Indeed.

Dad wiggled his brows.

Striding away dramatically in the tiniest burrow you ever saw. No self-respecting bunny rabbit would live in one so small. Yet here we are, crawling over each other in the West Village. Paying for the extraordinary privilege of residing in Manhattan by living in a Wonderland rabbit hole. An historic 1835 most desirable high rent hole.

Striding away creaking the worn old hardwood floors is heaps of fun in a one-BR apt, WBF, AC, casement windows, floor-through, but don't move fast. We tumbled and snuggled in my perfect *one*-person apartment. Also one bath: Did you go to *sleep* in there? we each holler once a week.

They say all women Over a Certain Age want to get married. A total lie! And can't find a man: media squeak-squawk.

Marriage was *not* on my agenda. Marriage=control. Brady belongs to a sex I don't trust. Though I trusted him. I think. With marriage, they turn from courtiers to commandants. From sweet angel honey lovers to, Do me, baby. Oh no, not me!

Sex and theology, plus cooking. We entertain. Oh yes, just like grownups. We *entertain*. With Faye and Teo, we jammed thirty of my beloved hateful colleagues into here during holiday break for Brady's baked ham and yams and green pea/olive salad and chocolate truffle cake. Teo couldn't believe he did it all.

Faye said, You made out, Alicia. A cook!

He won't let me in the kitchen, I said.

Lucky old you.

Faysie, he insists we get married.

Alicia, listen to boss lady. *Always* marry a cook.

Two months passed. One day Brady said, I may not be able to stay if we don't get married.

What on earth?

I want to be married, Alicia. If you don't—

Let me think about it. Ex-priests, seminarians, monks make great husbands. They're so deliriously happy to have sex—sex without guilt—monogamous sex—that they wouldn't dream of straying. I think.

Brady bolts out the door to work Saturdays for tax season. In his jeans because Saturday is Dress Down Day. Brady earns big bucks from January 15 to April 15.

Have you thought about it? he said April 16.

I strolled through the floor-through and back. I've decided. Okay. If you'll do it all.

Ah ha ha! Brady picked me up and swung me around and yahooed and yelped and we danced, singing, I get no kick from champagne,/ Flying so high....

Brady stopped. In a Catholic church?

Oh! Of course.

Do it all meant: proving to the Roman Catholic diocese he had never been married and proving my marriage and divorce was civil, not in church, retrieving our birth certificates, and my marriage and divorce papers.

I'll do it all, Brady said.

I was amazed Brady trusted me since I was so profoundly untrustworthy in matters of men. When young I thought nothing of writing three mad love letters to plan my summer—one to Eloy in Spain, one to Timmie in London, and one to Lalo in Mexico. I had my choice of replies, which I judged by their sincerity. And nearby beaches, mountains, scenic bliss.

Finally Brady's insane trustfulness, his good dog qualities, made me loyal and trustworthy. Because I couldn't bear to disappoint such an adoring eye. But was he really trustworthy or a Texas bullshitter who'd say anything? A Bohemian Czech-Bavarian German bullshitter. Ms. Super Wasp, he calls me because I overwork. Brady loves to make up True Tales and spin them.

Tacitus' *Germania*, finally I read it to discover Brady's sneaky characteristics. In two hundred AD Germans were loud, rowdy, carousing drunks, egalitarian, fierce warriors and monogamously married, unlike salacious Romans, said Tacitus, who knew. Just like Brady today! Monogamous. Hmm. Big bark but no bite. Hmm.

I can feel sexuality beginning to surge through my body. Like a plant that's been dormant, springing through the moist earth and winding rivulets of my body. Awakening lilacs in the dead land, as our Eliot said, in cruel April. By now I, Alicia, had fallen so in love with Brady that I marveled at his height, his gorgeous legs and butt, his near-nimble brain. Every year that man is with you, said Faye, he gets better looking.

Brady was madly in love with his dick, Juanito Bonito. Juanito Bonito, the name of his dick, and Brady were totally symbiotic, wild about each other. I wouldn't dream of breaking up this romance, as I benefitted so from it. Both had to focus on me. I'd be married to both.

Brady did it all, in the Mexican Catholic Church because we summer in San Miguel. Off to the *Parroquia* to be quizzed, submit to character examination. The *Parroquia*, the pink iced missile of a neogothic parish church that dominates the Jardín.

Our witnesses were Faye and Teófilo who bought a summer house here.

My darling Magali, of Lana Lujo, another witness, photographed the grand arrival, and Amparo and Herb appeared, all of us looking proper. Brady wore his Austin Reed double breasted blue blazer and I'm in, of all things, a skirt and polite low pumps.

We wait in an anteroom facing a dark tunnel through which we enter the *Parroquia* office. First, we write where we've lived since birth. Our witnesses testify they know us to be *solteros*, though in my case *divorciada*. Faye swears she's my New York friend and Teo that he's known me since he'd been with Faye.. Amparo testifies she's known me for fifteen years, since I first stayed at the popular hotel. Nobody is more respected in town than devout Amparo. Magali, whom I've known through two marriages, testifies she's known me for twelve years and Brady for eight years, since he first came to San Miguel. The *notario* stands behind a high imposing desk/wall and records this, as Padre Rey translates our English into Spanish for him. Portly amicable Otomi Padre Reynaldo Tapia, in his long black skirt, gives the English Mass his own incomprehensible twist on Sunday at Nuestra Señora de La Salud.

When they ask my age, blushing I whisper the secret to Padre Rey, who blushes, and repeats the dire charge to the Notary, who also blushes. We sign the huge book, which is tilted sideways for my left hand. Brady and I were escorted into a private office where the *Cura*, Padre José Bautista, waited in his long white skirt. The door firmly closed behind us, we were seated on the outskirts of his immense desk. Facing us was a huge *Sagrada Biblia* on which we placed our right hands, swearing to tell the whole truth. The previous information was solemnly repeated and solemnly sworn to. Brady has presented them his birth, baptism and confirmation documents, as well as my birth, marriage and divorce documents. They worry briefly over not having my baptism records. You can phone my parents, I offer jovially.

Padre Rey says to me, You understand a Catholic marriage is for life?

I admit I do.

Then he asks, You are *voluntarily* marrying this man?

And I wonder myself.

When he asks Brady if he's given this a great deal of thought, Brady replies, I've been thinking about it for five years.

I, Alicia, am still astounded he trusts *me* enough to carry it through.

Then the white haired informal *Cura*, a people-priest like Padre Rey, asks if I agree to raise the children Catholic. *Si hay milagro*, and I laughingly agree. If there's a miracle and a second virgin birth. We all laugh, since I'm passing childbearing age, and have only to deal with Brady's childishness. As he does with mine.

Then they phone Brady's mother in Texas, Brady's Bohemian Czech mother, Annie Luksovsky Shiner Witzkoske, who speaks even less Spanish than the priests' looping lariat English. Annie confirms that indeed her son has never married. Tell Annie hello, I say. Annie says hello to me. We are not allowed to speak to her. They are much impressed with Brady's mentor, who induced him into seminary, Father Jerome Stowell, and request his address. They are pleased he knows me too.

Since my graduate school marriage was civil, not religious, it doesn't count with Catholics. Hence I'm eligible. This projected church marriage also doesn't count with Mexican civil authorities, whose Revolution decreed only civil marriages legal. In the eyes of God, says Brady. As I believe God is in the imagination, as did poet Wallace Stevens, I'm going along with this. We were released and told our papers would go to the Bishop in Celaya for his decision. We took our testifiers to the Fragua for drinks and dancing.

We heard no more about it and I hoped everyone had forgotten. Brady and I went back to New York for the school year.

A friend of Mary Rockefeller called and offered us her San Miguel house for the summer—swimming pool, staff, fifteen hundred dollars a month. I demurred. Mary—whose husband Lawrence had been governor of Kansas and whose son Jay is longtime Senator from West Virginia—and some friends had bought mansions early on.

By the time we returned to San Miguel the next summer I'd decided *never* to marry him. Brady had gotten roaring, raging, crotchety. His family, the Bavarian side, was given to hissy fits. Abrupt violent explosions of temper out of nowhere, over next to nothing. When I told him he was driving too close to the edge of the road, *explosion!*

Don't talk to me when I'm driving, you bitch. I'll wreck the car.

You'll wreck it anyway if you go over the edge, I pointed out.

Don't interrupt me, he screamed. I never get a chance to talk. You never listen to me. You have to have your way. Always, *your* way.

At first I was shocked into silence. I learned he wouldn't shut up till I screamed louder than he did. *What's wrong with you, you toad-fucker? Let me out of this car!*

Silence. Beat, beat. Thirty seconds pass. How's Love Britches? He picks up my hand and kisses it.

Mother warned me you have no emotional control, I said. I'm listening now.

Give me a kiss, Alpha Female. He starts singing, I Get a Kick Out of You.

You love to do that, I said. Shove rage out the door into me. Now you're free and sassy and I'm miserable. *Fuck off, asshole.*

The permission to marry arrived at La Salud and Brady made formal arrangements with Padre Rey to marry us. One year later.

Sorry, I said, I've changed my mind. I will never marry any fool with a temper like yours. *Never!*

But I didn't care because we had produced the *San Miguel Review, 1989.* Marty Cramer, Charlie Kuschinski and I chose the stories and poems. It was a sturdy paperback with a wild figurative painting by Marty on the cover. In this lofty production were poems by Pulitzer Prize winning poet, W.D. Snodgrass, called one of the six best poets in the English language by the *New York Times.* Snodgrass and wife Kathy wintered in San Miguel. Also Charlie's story, *"Boys,"* and six poems by Terry Burke, including *"Harris County Jail."* My story was about Faye and Teófilo's romance, called *"The Naked Gringa."* I'll have to ask Faye if I got it right. Why did I write it? Because Faye never would. Or because I wish something that romantic and strange had happened to me?

The only San Miguel paperback ever published, it was a sensation and we were all very proud of it. If I could write, what did I care about oaf Brady?

About every three or four months I decided to kick him out of my apartment and change the locks. He raged like a lunatic, accusing me of being every kind of evil stupid nasty bitch, advancing on me, frightening me intentionally with his big body. Male rage—screaming testosterone. He never touched me.

The fish needs more white wine and fewer onions, I said.

Don't criticize my cooking! I work like a *slave*. I'm not your maid! *You* do it or we don't eat. Throws down the spatula, sits on sofa. Now, apologize.

Like a child. I apologize.

Shouts, screams, You don't mean it. I want respect! You always want everything your way. You never listen to me!

I read: male emotional equipment hasn't changed significantly since those good old hunter/gatherer days. As if a volcano inside him kept building, fuming and burning till the tiniest impetus caused it to blow. A rash of aftershocks for a half hour or so then dormant again for months and months.

Brady refused couple therapy. "You're the one who needs it," he said. "You don't hear yourself." Hm, maybe.

Then for months and months Brady would be cheerful, playful, darling, and I'd forget. Brady possessed every extreme unmatched characteristic with no middle ground. Bi-polar? Who knows? He was far angrier than I and far far more joyful.

Repeat, I will not marry you. I want you *out of my life*.

Brady grinned, I won't go.

Brady didn't complain. He campaigned. Mr. Adorable, butter wouldn't melt, kiss my feet. Actually, pick up each foot as I lay back on the bed and kiss softly, repeatedly. Special treats, flowers, rented a house for us with space.

I ignored him and studied my research project, my box of books by and on medieval literary women. Writings of early abbesses, especially Hildegarde de Bingen; mystics, Margery a Kempe among them; Sor Juana Inéz de la Cruz, the seventeenth century Mexican nun; curanderas, witches from the Renaissance backward in time, Sappho and the Amazons, to the most ancient goddesses, pre-Christian and pre-Columbian.

Brady was so adorable I fell madly in love with him again. As soon as he realized that, he became a cockatoo. *He* had the power, he thought, because I, poor Alicia, was helplessly enamored of him. Silly fool!

Get to heel, Brady, I said, get to heel.

Brady roared explosively. Brady's laughter is loud enough to detonate a bomb. You took me in and loved me, that's why I'm vain. It's all your fault.

Your vanity is like a desert flower that bloomed after forty years and got outrageous. Years without rain, then—

That's right!

Now you think you're God almighty.

I am. You love me. I can't help it.

No emotional control.

At dusk Brady escorted me back to the spot on Calle Relox where we originally met. There in the street, he knelt on one knee and proposed. Will Ms. Alicia do me the honor of marrying me?

People stared.

Both knees, I said.

Both knees it was. He took my hand and gazed up at me.

Maybe, I said.

Dear Mother and Dad,
Brady and I are getting married here on Sept.
30th. The *boda* (wedding) will be in English with
a Mass at Nuestra Señora de la Salud Church,
Tres Ave Marías Chapel. This shocks me but it's
time for commitment to the man I live with and
love. Now, both your daughters will be married,

Leila and I both to practicing Catholics, of all
things. But since you declared him my White
Knight, what can I do? We're thrilled and will
phone, etc....

Besos and love,

Alicia

In Nuestra Señora de la Salud, a brilliant silver sunburst
of clouds surrounds the white garbed Virgin with her fancy dancing skirt stiffly extended on each side. Gold etches
billowy clouds with a gold sun spray surrounded by angel-
ic nymphs. In Tres Ave Marías Chapel, the altar features a
bare-chested Jesús with a low Aztec toga slung on his hips
in pale blue folds, wearing a white crown. The Virgin Mother
holds the cross, with St. Joseph on the other side and golden
sunlit angels around the panoply. White lilies mass in earthen
pots before the altar.

With Padre Rey, we enter with our three witnesses and
their mates, Amparo and Magali and Teófilo, all three Catholic—though Teo has lapsed—taking photos. We wanted our *boda*
small instead of festive. They insisted on toting bags of rice to
toss at us afterward. Mexicans came in to sit and pray, among
them very poor old señoras in worn aprons and faded rags of
rebozos. Young señoras with *bebés* and small children, a few campesinos in humble clothes, weathered sombreros beside them.
No one middleclass, of course.

We're blessed, we kneel, we read. I edit Ecclesiastes.

...All the rivers run into the sea, yet the sea is not full. Unto
the place

from whence the rivers come, thither they return again.

To every thing there is a season.

A time to be born and a time to die,

A time to mourn and to dance,

A time to keep silence and a time to love.

Brady read Psalm 23—Yea, though I walk—and from the Catholic missal.

While we knelt, Padre Rey's priestly advice to us, at our age, was to warn us our major problems would be with health and money, and we must succour each other in illness and hard times. When I asked him earlier if he was going to tell me to obey my husband, he'd laughed, and said, Oh no, we took that out years ago.

Richer or poorer, in sickness or in health, we agreed to it all.

Brady placed a gold band on my finger and I placed a gold band on his.

Padre Rey pronounced us husband and wife, we kissed with wet eyes.

We kissed Padre Rey who embraced us both.

A poor señora held out her hand and I gave her money, another begged and Brady gave her some pesos. Our three witnesses at the massive church door tossed rice at us as we stepped out. As the rice fell and scattered, poor people crawled between us and scooped up the rice in their hands and aprons, dropped it into the little plastic bags that had been discarded, scooped and scraped till every grain of rice was gone. On their hands and knees, *los pobres*, after every single grain.

We took our witnesses and their mates, Magali and Chuy, Amparo and Herb, and Teófilo with Faysie, to the Terraza Campestre for comida. Happily, Magali and her number two, Chuy, seem solidly clenched. Teo and Faye are perfectly mated; they are the same. We opened our bottle of Viuda de Romero tequila and slugged it to calm down. We loved San Miguel, the Sierras, the people. Through scarlet and magenta *bugambilia* on the yellow terrace, I still saw *los pobres* on their knees scraping their knuckles on the stones grasping for rice.

Before the *boda*, photos show Brady with sheer fear in his eyes. Afterward he was gleeful. I was proud of Brady for trusting me, and of *me* for daring the same. Being married to Brady is like being married to my lover, my father, my mother, sisters, plus a raging maniac, and a baby boy. Each emerging unannounced, uncalled for, inexcusable.

You don't hear yourself, says he. But I forgive you.

La Casa De Serena

Hank and Serena and I pick our way over the cobble-stones to Serena's house. She invited us for a special visit because Hank decided to help her financially. Serena is our upstairs maid at the hotel, a timid and docile Chichimeca with long glossy black hair, arched nose and almond eyes, very pretty. Hank the school teacher is a rough handsome Kentuckian of Scot-Irish lineage, who wears a rakish Panama to cover his bald spot. Brady has to work this summer in New York so I'm staying at the hotel.

"Alicia, will you translate?" Serena asked.

Serena chats with Mexican graciousness, that delicacy of contact that is the soul's essence, an innate spirit that lightens and makes you feel human. Stroll the narrow *calles* and people you've seen once say Buenos días, Buenas tardes. All you have to do is smile to see a face open. Mexico is like the South. People warm the streets.

In summers Serena and I gossip about men. *Cuándo vas a con-seguirme un nuevo novio?* Serena says. When are you going to get me a new sweetheart? *Tomas mi esposo, Brady. Vamos a intercambi-ar,* I reply. Take my husband, Brady. Let's exchange.

We turn into an alley off Prolongación Aldama and reach Serena's house. Serena's house is one dark room with a double bed and a single bed, the door the only light and air. Concrete sides, thatch roof. Outside a narrow wooden shed with sloping corrugated roof not over five feet high, where her father sleeps. Dirt passageway and tiny low roofed kitchen shed to the back. Both sheds are made of small pieces of wood and metal, held by rocks, that a real wind would destroy. Everything crumbles.

We open our *refrescos*. We brought *guayaba*. Salud, I say, wondering what's between her and Hank.

Tell her, says Hank, how happy I am to be able to help her out.

I tell Serena who smiles and blushes, as if she hardly dares believe it. Doesn't dare glance at Hank who grins benevolently. What does he want? she wonders.

This is my bed, says Serena. I sleep here with my four children. My brother and his wife and their *niño* sleep in the other bed.

How much a month? I wonder for this hovel.

Three hundred fifty pesos, she says. About thirty-eight dollars.

But what do they pay you at the hotel? I ask, as if I didn't know it was minimum wage. All the employees earn minimum wage, even if they've worked there fifteen years.

Mi sueldo es one hundred ninety pesos, she says, a week. About twenty-one dollars, for six days. I tell Hank.

During Serena's twelve years there, the hotel rates have jumped from two hundred dollars to four hundred dollars a month. No longer the best deal in the Western world.

Tell Serena, says Hank, I will send her money as long as I work and have health. Forty dollars every month.

Serena barely dares to glance at Hank then lowers her eyes in tears. More than her rent—forty dollars.

I don't care what's between them, I think it's noble. Hank is on his fourth wife. Maybe he needs a summer mistress.

What does your brother do? I ask Serena.

He works at La Mamacita as a waiter. Most popular restaurant, most popular hotel. And they live here.

Two of her children, Ignacio, now thirteen, and Sarita, now eleven, greet us with shy courtesy. Sarita washed her hair and put on her pink company dress. Ignacio, who has that hungry burro look of the poor, shakes hands with us politely. They have manners, as even the poorest Mexicans do.

Ignacio, says Serena, now you can go to *Secondaria* because we can pay for clothes and books. Serena says this to test Hank, to see if he'll snatch it all away.

Mama, I'll pass the exam, I'll study and study! Color comes into his face and his eyes light, as he glances at Hank and me.

The exam is August 15th. Children in town compete for places in middle school or junior high. Those with money get tutored. Serena says Ignacio is a good student and I pray it's so.

Tell her, says Hank enthusiastically, I want to help her because she is my sister.

When I tell her, Serena weeps silently turning her head aside. Having never been treated fairly, generosity is almost a threat. Of its ending. Of being punished for being singled out. Is it a trick? How will she have to pay for this?

Yesterday afternoon at the hotel she had on her tight jeans and flouncy Spanish blouse ready to go home. Hank approached her. They'd been flirting and she knew if he wanted her, she couldn't resist. She'd left her husband eight long months ago. Tall slim gringo with blue eyes who moved nicely. There at the private end of the upstairs terrace, they moved forward as if they'd swallow each other in a carnivorous embrace. Serena's arms were ready to go around his neck and Hank's large hands clutched her waist.

Then Hank did something strange, as if a light had struck him. Hank stepped back and released her, looked up as if he heard a voice that stopped him.

Serena, he said, I must not—you are my sister. I must help you because you are my true sister. He gave her waist a little shake. Yes, I'll do it!

Serena dropped her arms, disappointed. What did he mean?

Apparently, this. How can I thank you, señor? Serena says to me, and I to Hank. How she misses her *young* husband, the early years. Not the brute she left.

Only by caring for your fine family, says Hank. Tell her I have two grown children, boy and girl, from two of my marriages. Floride is number four.

I tell her, grinning. Hank has been very busy.

Will he forget back in California? Gringo enthusiasm fades at home. Several Norteamericanas said they'd send for her to be their maid. None did.

What happened with that sweet husband of yours? Serena had told me how she loved to sleep cuddled up beside him, how she loved to touch him. They'd been together since they were both fifteen.

About a year ago he started drinking, says Serena. When he couldn't get jobs. He was an assistant *albanil*—bricklayer. Then he was so borracho nobody would hire him. Before he drank, he'd stay home and care for the children. He was much better at it than I am. It's harder for men to get work. But then, the *mescal*. He was always in rage, he screamed, roared, he —. So eight months ago we separated and I came back to this house—Papá's house—with my four kids. The youngest spend the day with *mi suegra*—mother-in-law.

Serena's mother died of breast cancer when she was a girl, I recall.

Oh, Serena, poor Serena, says Hank. What luck that I'm here to help.

Serena smiles with Delphic solemnity at me and almost at Hank. Where is his wife? she whispers to me.

Hank explains that Floride doesn't like San Miguel and we look at him in wonderment. We *love* San Miguel.

Alicia, says Serena, por favor, say nothing to the Señor about this. Last year Serena washed clothes for a few pesos after hours for guests. The hotel owner got furious that she was shirking her work, and put a stop to it.

Of course not, I say.

Serena had only wanted two children to feed. She had an IUD inserted but it became painful so she had it removed. Geraldo, now five, and Teresa, now three, were born. She had the IUD replaced and became anemic, very weak, and worked with difficulty. I always share my meat from the hotel restaurant because the hotel only feeds the waitresses. Also I feel her anemia is partly due to lifelong protein deprivation. The working poor subsist on tortillas and beans. We upstairs guests leave clothes and shoes behind for Serena. Sunhats, vases, small rugs, lotions, lipsticks, plus tips.

Hank takes photos of all of us, which he'll send Serena.

Tell her, says Hank, that my prosperity comes to me through the grace of God and that is why I wish to share it with my sister, Serena. I'm so pleased she will use it to educate her family. As long as there is breath in my body, I will send her money.

Hank seems ecstatic in his love for Serena and her family. Although he can speak no Spanish and she can't pronounce his name. *Jaunk,* she says.

Gracias por visitar mi pobre casita, Serena thanks us, and says the house may be sold so her father is looking for another. But it's hard to find a place they can afford.

Thank God, I said, you have a job.

We climb the hill to see a new house. Serena's slow sure Mother Earth movements seem to emanate from the universe around us, the whirling sky and craggy rock. I see her walking here a thousand—five thousand—years ago when there were only mountains and thick growth over the crags.

She holds Ignacio's hand and I hold Sarita's. Hank hauls Sarita up a steep ledge. Serena and Ignacio and Sarita walk us back to Parque Juarez.

The children love to walk in the afternoon, she says. She presses my hand then his. *Mi casa es siempre suya.* We kiss cheeks goodbye.

Wait, says Hank, and finally hauls a money envelope out of his pocket. If the children—God forbid—get ill and need medical help, take this letter to the new medical center, and I will pay for it. They know me.

Serena nods with her majestic patience, as if she will accept anything good or bad without surprise.

I meant to get gifts but I didn't have time, says Hank.

Serena takes the envelope politely without looking down or pressing the bills inside.

The children scamper ahead. Serena says quietly, Alicia, the children say they never want another father.

So then I knew how bad it had been.

We hug goodbye. Hank gives her a sisterly squeeze.

As we walk back to the hotel, I feel shamefully rich.

I knew the house would be poor, says Hank, but I didn't know *how* poor. Why does she think the hotel owner will be upset?

Because she's not being paid enough to live on, and they know it. The warmth of her children is Serena's only solace.

Eyes asparkle, Hank says, blushing, It makes me deliriously excited to do this, to actually make a *difference* for a fine person like Serena. Do you know why I'm doing it?

No.

Because God told me to. Hank turns to me, proud exaltation brimming his face, When I went to seduce her, Alicia—I knew I could, she was so sexy, those hugging jeans —God appeared to me and spoke, You must *not* do this. You must help her. She is your sister.

Serena has a patron because God has a believer.

All my prosperity, everything I have, says Hank, comes to me by the grace of God.

Hank never would forget. Over the years he would pay for the education of all four children. Even as he grew older and so did she, Hank never forgot his sister, Serena. Even when he stopped coming down because all he did in San Miguel was get drunk.

Every summer I write her letters to Hank and translate his to her. Like most of her age and class, Serena can't read or write.

Hank always asks after each child by name. Sometimes I phone from New York for her or for him.

After eight years he bought her a TV, she tells me ecstatically. By then Serena lives in Malanquín, a big government housing project, designed to look like an adobe pueblo, on the high hill facing town. By age eighteen, Ignacio, and Sarita at sixteen, the oldest boy and girl, are in Tucson, he working construction and she as a maid. Both wetbacked up, paying their *coyote* to drop them in the desert.

Retired, Hank married his fifth wife, a *Filipina*, and moved to Manila. He forgot his sister Serena.

Serena has only two *niños* left at home. There are gray streaks in her hair. Then Serena is *embarazada* again. I offer to arrange for her to have a legal abortion in the States.

No, Alicia, she shyly demurs, I couldn't do that. My children are my life.

She smiles and primps her short curly black permanent. She's washed away the gray. Her eyes shine.

Do you ever hear from Hank? I ask.

No. He does not write me anymore.

I sigh. He moved to the other side of the world, to a new life, I say. The phone was disconnected years ago.

Serena has three more children—seven in all—before she confesses to me she has a new man, a younger man. She is forty-four, Javier is thirty-five, and they've been together for eight years. Javier works construction in Phoenix. He bought her a phone and pays phone bills so she can talk to her children in the States. She bears Javier's *niños* so he is her *señor*.

Mexican men won't stay with a barren woman. They decided three was enough, and she had her tubes tied.

Solamente un problema, Serena says. He wants very much to marry me. I told him I married once in the church for life. I would not marry again.

Entonces, mi vida, I say, you will keep him for life.

She gives me her sly holy smile. *Yo sé.* I know.

We grasp hands and circle with our new summer chant:

Cada año más vieja, cada año más mejor.

Every year older, every year better.

Tres Por Tres Por Tres

3 X 3 X 3

"Tess, you don't mind if I take off with José Manuel, do you?" asked Clarice, the quiet one. "With your friend coming?" Clarice was wild about José Manuel.

Tawny Tess' head sank into her hands. "I wish my 'friend' wasn't coming." Athletic Tess, all-American girl, was having a heated affair with Hector Aciles.

Both women had made Maruja, their Spanish teacher, their advisor. "Maruja, his sexual vibrations were so strong, they drove me totally ape, insane, to seduce him," said Tess. "We spend every afternoon in bed as well as night. Maruja, he's the most marvelous lyrical lover, I'm mad about Hector Aciles, and it's tearing me apart. My lover of two years is coming to town in a *week*."

"You'd better watch out," warned Clarice.

"In a week Olga will be here," said Tess. "What can I do about Olga?"

Maruja called summer rainy season Schoolteachers' Quarter because they were everywhere. They clambered over *las ruinas*, tried out painting and Mexican lovers, studied Spanish and weaving and potting. Tess and Clarice were schoolteachers from San Jose, California.

The most naive gringas at the hotel, thought Maruja, the artist who was their Spanish teacher. Like Mexicanas. Like herself. Maruja ran around with a *mezclada* of musicians, artists, antique smugglers, dope dealers, local teachers, and layabouts living on invisible incomes.

Maruja had come here from the northwest, Zacatecas, to *Bellas Artes*, the national art school, in this sinful resort town. Every week her mama wrote her to come home and marry "before you're so old no man wants you." Guiltily, Maruja refused. Mama did not know about Sean Suárez. Now Maruja taught Spanish to tourists and met the world.

Tess and Clarice stayed *in* at night the whole month of July. Diligently they studied Spanish by the swimming pool at siesta time, as Maruja struggled through the icy turquoise water. Maruja was pleased they struggled to learn Español, as she had to master English and swimming. Most Mexicans don't swim; they soak in hot springs.

Mexican single men and women came to the hotel now, in twos and threes, and city couples with well dressed small children. Also big French and German groups, occasional Asians. Some weeks Mexicans actually outnumbered the foreigners, who'd discovered this rose washed stone hacienda laced with tumultuous gardens. Flowering lavender crawled up trees. Lizards slithered down walls. Bugambilia sprouted from every crevice.

The Sacrificial *Cenote*, Maruja called the swimming pool, because you climbed high pyramid steps like those at Chichen Itza to reach it. The water was too cold for Tess and Clarice who took Yolanda's *Aeróbicas*. Californians don't swim; they take aerobics. Diving in was Maruja's sacrifice. Maruja with her serene poster eyes, her doe eyes and beige silk skin, was determined to stay in shape. Maruja's flesh had that poreless perfection unique to Latinas. Hands smooth and tapered. No freckles, veins, joints showed, as they do on *gringas.*.

Then José Manuel and Hector Aciles arrived at the hotel, young men the equal of Tess and Clarice in timidity. They all looked somewhat alike, thought Maruja, and that was because José Manuel and Hector Aciles were schoolteachers too, from Mexico City. All four dressed and talked and looked modest, sensible, and quietly humorous, the two Mexican men in their twenties like Maruja, the two gringas in their thirties. When they began going out together, so Maruja thought, it will take ladies and gentlemen of this sort longer than August to work up to romance.

While Maruja waited for her viejito Sean Suárez, the Tex Mex-Irish guitarist, to join her, she strummed her guitar alone. Sean was playing a gig in Santa Fe. Maruja made Assemblages of found materials which she painted like votive objects, hanging odd bits from her clothes or her shiny cascading black hair. Maruja liked to feel *bohemia pero fiel*—bohemian but faithful. She studied Nahuatl, using pictographic symbols in paintings along with her found objects.

José Manuel the string bean strolled with Clarice, slight blonde and freckled, who'd come from France as a girl to

California, he with a gaunt Don Quixote innocence matching her unmarked visage. Clarice taught high school French. Hector Aciles, the handsomer, shorter and more muscular, strolled with Tess. Maruja called tawny Tess the all-American girl because she was stocky and smiley and looked like she taught Girls' Sports. Which she did. Both boys were Mexico City pale, beige skin lightened by pollution hiding the sun. Smog was turning *los chilangos* white.

Maruja lost track of them totally when she met Hans, the married German geneticist. Whose marriage, of course, was breaking up, of course. Hans loved Espana, and came here because he heard this Mexican mountain town had El Greco skies like Toledo and crumbling stone like Segovia. Hans had pedaled here on a bike he bought in Guanajuato, over the mountains in his lederhosen with his great Teutonic trees of legs. Hans was fascinated by exotic Latinas, so graciously unlike Aryans.

Hans kissed Maruja's hands which were as supple as a benediction. He kissed her neck to inhale the delicacy of her aroma there. "You're fated to adore me, and I you," twinkled Hans, golden god of the Huns, to Maruja, dark lady of the sonnets.

"You're a comedian, Hans," said Maruja. "No, no, no. For the hundredth time."

With Hans at dusk, as huge flocks of grackles swooped down from all the hills to the Jardín, and into rounded trees so lush-leafed not a bird could be seen. While light lasted, a thousand birds chirped away in a symphonic roar at their levitating Happy Hour. But Hans was unexpectedly caring and patient, and lulled her with talk of the great world.

When he had only five days left in town, Maruja, wildly resisting, gave in. An earthquake of passion—a *terremoto*—erupted in Maruja, new and devastating. Hans left her in ruins. He also left her his bike.

"I'll dream of my love on my seat," Hans had twinkled. Hans was a bit crazy, thought Maruja.

Reeling with guilt after Hans' departure, Maruja confessed to Tess and Clarice at breakfast, and became their confidante. Quiet Clarice, though French born, was having her first extra-marital affair with José Manuel, she at thirty-nine with two teenage kids.

"He's about twenty-nine," said Clarice.

All-American Tess winked at Maruja. Both knew José Manuel was twenty-one.

"Of course," said Clarice, "my husband has had affairs. But I feel guilty." So untouched looking was blonde small-boned tidy-featured Clarice, that the age difference didn't show. Maruja had noticed that older Norteamericanas and younger men didn't seem as far apart in age as older North American men and younger women. Gringas stay young a long time.

"A little *igualidad* with your *libertad*," Maruja advised Clarice.

"The truth is," blushed Clarice, "I feel guilty because I don't feel guilty. Not at all."

"Lucky for you." Maruja wondered if she should go to Confesssion again. The gold crowned Virgin in blue in her ivory filigree niche at the Parroquia, so pure in spirit, rankled Maruja. A sure sign of guilt.

"Now, Maruja," said Clarice, "José Manuel's asked me to travel with him to the beaches for two weeks. Should I go?" Both women viewed Maruja as experienced in local wisdom and lore.

"He seems trustworthy and kind," said Maruja, still sighing over Hans. "If you want to, GO, have fun. *Vaya!*"

"They're both vouched for," said Tess. "We met the Super-intendent of their school in town. He and his wife have a house here. Did I tell you," said jaunty Tess, "I was an Aztec princess in a previous life?"

"Then you'll have to worship me," Maruja replied, "as I was Coatlicue, mother of the Aztec gods." They spluttered with laughter.

Maruja wished Mexico thrilled her like it did Tess and Clarice. Puerto Escondido, Zihuatanejo, Yelapa, Bucerias, they selected beaches like magic spells. Much to be said for travel, sighed Maruja. No wonder she couldn't resist Hans the German geneticist: twelve days in Munich, travel right here in town.

Hans had thrilled her with the opening of the Berlin Wall, East-West German unification, the university atmosphere, ski mountains, jobs, apartments. Why, she'd feel almost at home in Bavaria. Maruja longed for money to travel. She'd been to Texas and New Mexico only, with Sean Suárez, her *viejito*.

Hans had been enchanted by this high heaving land. Hans claimed, of course, he'd leave his wife except she was too fragile, emotionally, of course. Maruja didn't even bother to listen to this, knowing various local *Casa Chicas*—established mistress with whom the husband sires his illegitimate line—at home in Zacatecas too. Briefly she wondered about her own father. No, no, she reddened, not possible.

Tawny Tess' high spirits suddenly turned to loud sobs. "Maruja, what can I do? With Olga on her way. I'm in love with Hector Aciles—totally truly in love."

"When is she coming?"

"Olga will be here tomorrow."

Olga arrived at the hotel, big and burly and furious that Tess had betrayed her with a man: the enemy. Maruja was more shocked by Olga's appearance than by the fact that she was a woman. While Tess was hefty but feminine, Olga was a real *marimacha*, low and fat in the haunches, short legged, with a tough wary face. Her nose ring seemed to snort. Her dark crew cut featured three earrings on her right ear. What could anyone as sweet-tempered and sexy and well, regular, as Tess see in Olga? Olga looked implacable.

Maruja heard them fighting in their room.

"I'm sorry, Olga, I can't, I just can't." A muffled scream, a sob.

"You're a traitor. You didn't tell me you're bisexual."

"I'm not," wailed Tess, "Hector's different."

A loud thumping noise, a wail, then silence.

Next morning at breakfast Tess' face was mottled, her arm bruised. She sat with Maruja, and Olga joined Clarice at a far table. Jaunty Tess was silent, looked crazed, asked Maruja if she could come to her room to talk.

"I need a drink, strong." She shook.

Maruja poured her tequila *derecha* at eleven AM.

"It's not fair," moaned Tess. "Olga had an affair with another woman, after we'd been living together a year. At dances, I had to sit and suffer while she and Heidi wrapped around each other." Tess said she'd been in the lesbian scene ten years. "I'm a radical feminist," she said. "I'd just as soon punch out most men as look at them."

Hiding her amazement, Maruja said, "The point is, you're attracted to another person, not a sex. That's why she's angry."

"I can't sleep with her, I only want Hector," wailed Tess. "He's so gentle, he hates macho stuff—the dominating family man like his father, my father. My father turned me off men, all right. He used to smack me, for nothing. When I was little, he threw me against the wall. When I left at twenty, he tried to...." Tess sobbed, "That's why I studied Phys Ed—sports, to you. To get strong."

That night Tess went with Hector Aciles and Olga's nose ring snorted like an angry bull. Olga forbade Tess to see Hector Aciles.

Next day another tequila after breakfast with Maruja, who sipped manzanilla tea. "What do you mean, she forbade you?"

"She gets, well, physical when she's angry," Tess groaned. "I want to quit my job, and go to Mexico City, and have an affair with Hector. I don't care what she says."

Sensible Maruja said, "Tell me what you see in Olga, Tess."

"She's a woman, for God sake. I like the married feeling with her. Look what she's had to overcome. She's ugly, my poor dear." Tess sniffled. "But every six months or so, I have to sleep with a man or I'll go crazy. Hector Aciles is the first one it's mattered with. Maybe because I'm thirty-two. The old biological clock, I don't know."

Maruja was in the same position. Still dreaming about Hans the Bavarian with her old man, Sean, coming next week. Now in her previous-life dreams, she was Brunnhilde deep in the forest, Brunnhilde wailing with passion, streaming along in her chariot. "How's sex with Olga, Tess?"

"Oh, you know, regular. We get it on about once a week. Olga's not too sexual and I like that. She's more, oh, domestic, maternal."

Tess had another tequila. "I never felt this way in my life, Maruja. I want to throw over everything and start a new life.

This isn't just an affair. It could destroy my whole world." Her longing, her tension, made Maruja ache for Hans.

Tess saw Hector Aciles again that night and didn't come back to her room. Outside on the terrace Olga stalked back and forth, moaning like a beast in pain. She didn't knock at Hector's door for the longest time. Finally Olga banged and hollered, banged and hollered to silence, not knowing Hector had moved their love nest to another hotel. Yet dutiful Tess returned in the dead of night to the room she shared with Olga. The row the next dawn was so loud it woke half the hotel.

At breakfast Maruja warned Olga and Tess they'd lose their room if they didn't, *Como se dice,* Cool It.

Señora Amparo, the owner, entered the dining room and marched to Tess and Olga's table. "You will leave this hotel if there is ONE SOUND tonight," she said with wrathful gentility.

Neither woman replied. The next day and night were quiet. Tess stayed in with Olga, having explained the problem to Hector Aciles.

That night at La Mamacita, Maruja saw Hector Aciles, despondent, infinitely sad. What a blow it must be to this Mexican man's macho pride to know he had a rival who wasn't even male. Hector sat, arms crossed, Tres Equis untouched in front of him, surrounded by Peruvian flute buffs, unhearing. He caught Maruja's eye and bowed his head. Maruja sat beside him, patted his hand, murmured, "You must try, Hector. You must insist."

Next morning Olga looked considerably better, Tess quite subdued.

Tess came to Maruja's room to say a sudden goodbye. "Olga wants to leave today, before things get worse. I don't want you to think she's always like this." Tess whipped a snapshot of herself and Olga and parents from her wallet.

Maruja said, "Olga looks just like her father."

"That's my father," said Tess.

"Maybe that's the attraction," said Maruja, as Tess looked stunned. "Olga's alot like your father."

"You don't *know* that," said Tess, hurt.

A bad silence.

"What about Hector Aciles?"

"He fell apart when I told him. He's so upset, he's leaving, and I love him so much, I can't bear to lose him. I feel like they're pulling me apart with horses."

"Tess, I think you should spend time with Hector Aciles. To find out if he's a fantasía or if your feelings are real. Or you'll resent your defeat by Olga." Maruja's sage advice often surprised Maruja.

"That's what we're planning," Tess brightened. "A secret rendezvous this week in Mexico City. Olga's going to the Yucatan and I told her I'm flying home."

"Does she believe you?"

"Probably not."

"Suppose she tries to stop you?"

"I'll smash her!" Tess said. Then blushed.

Maruja felt a strange letdown when she saw Tess and Olga drive off. Because she liked Tess and would miss her? Or because gentle Hector Aciles was her countryman? Or because gringas had so many choices? Choices Mexicanas only dream of. José Manuel and Clarice had left the week before for their two-week spree. Hector Aciles disappeared quietly. Sad cars leaving.

Maruja waited for Sean, her Tex Mex-Irish viejito, the guitarist, strumming little airs of desire, which she transferred from Hans by going to Confession. By practicality. Maruja understood limitation, caution. She painted a burden of desire changing shape as it crossed the canvas. This started a whole new symbolism in Maruja's painting.

Sean had been almost a month with Maruja, playing with the flute group at La Mamacita, when a letter was shoved under the door. It was from Tess who wrote:

>...You won't believe this but Clarice left her husband and two kids and is living in Mexico City with José Manuel, teaching English as a second language.
>We practically overlapped.

>I stayed a whole month with Hector Aciles, loving every minute, till I got tired and began missing Olga ferociously. I told her if she ever laid a hand on me again, I'd clobber her and leave. She's much better behaved after a good scare. Less like my father, as you would say, but also, you see, Olga's like my dear mother.
>I'm just gay*—bless your straight bones.
>Hector was hurt. Everybody was hurt. Come see us in San Jose.
>
>Besos,

>*Except twice a year.
>
>Tess

There's a certain advantage in being a loyal, guilt-ridden *Mexicana bohemia ateísta Católica*, thought Maruja. You do less damage than the free and innocent fast-moving people from the North.

Then Maruja got her fourth letter from Hans the German geneticist. Hans had left his wife. I don't even want to hear about it, thought Maruja. Summer's over. Hans wondered if she could come to Munich for an extended visit; he could arrange the money for the travel.

Maruja wished she'd never come here, to this Mexican bohemia where she'd learned art, English, met the world, but never yet hurt anyone. She sat by the pool, pondering Han's letter. Now Maruja entered the free and open valley of choice and pain, the valley of the shadow of the gringas of the North.

Sean Suárez waved, as he loped toward her in his cowboy dude stride.

Maruja dove into the pool, to escape her guilt.

Sean would get over it. But if she hurt herself, how could she forgive that?

Hans could live without her, she well knew, on the other side of the world. If Hans hurts her, will she forgive him? She expanded, expaaaandiiing, flying, out out over the Atlantic.

Ambición

On *Indio Triste* live two handsome compadres who are amateur wrestlers who've appeared on local TV. Both taxi drivers, Angelito and Jesús, called Chucho, are great buddies who share the same ambición. A lofty ambición that only awaits opportunity. Angelito and Jesús want to be Hit Men.

They hear a *gringa* wants to get rid of her husband. A bummer and a *borracho*, Jane tells me, I want to get rid of him. Get my life back. Jesús and Angelito overhear this and discreetly follow Jane home.

Sombreros removed, both bow and explain that having overheard her desperation, they will undertake the job. They will get rid of Jane's husband for two hundred dollars.

What on earth do you mean? says Jane.

Chucho points an imaginary *pistola* at his own head and obligingly falls down.

Locos, Jane says as she slams the door. She phones me and I tell her to call Faye and Teófilo. What sort of joke is that? she asks.

Teo says they're poor to average wrestlers. But he doesn't know them. It must be their own joke because they like *gueras*. Mexican men are loco for blondes. Ask Teo.

Several days later Angelito and Chucho knock again. They figure they've given the Señora time to think it over, check them out.

Señora, we are at your service, says Angelito, whose baby face fits his name.

We won't even charge you for new *pistolas*, says Chucho, gazing with wonder at the wealth inside. The biggest TV he's ever seen, gold this, silver that, DVD, immense stereo, two huge computer setups. And that was just from the slit through the heavy carved wooden door.

Jane's green eyes narrow. Either this is somebody's inane joke or you boys are dangerous.

No, Señora, we aim to please, Chucho pleads. His chest expands and he works his wide muscled shoulders at her. Chucho looks like that *estrella del cine*, what's his name, the incredible looking one.

Jane slams the door, wondering if she should phone the *policía*. Who'll probably laugh, says Teófilo.

As men of ambición Angelito and Chucho don't give up. They decide their best plan may be to rob the Señora instead. Tie her down and have fun. But, *chingao*, they forgot her husband there in the house.

Next time, the boys are confronted by Jane's husband. They disappear fast, yelling Just for play, *chiste, chiste, chiste*. Joke, joke, joke.

Finally Jane gets rid of her husband. He moves out and goes home to Dallas.

Months pass. Chucho appears and apologizes, saying his attraction to Jane was too powerful and he figured some damn fool scheme would cause her to notice him. Could he possibly do some carpentry or painting for her?

This goes on for months till Jane lets him paint the interior patio wall.

You know how these things go. Before long, Chucho is her *novio* and finally her live-in boyfriend. This is the first time in his life Chucho has gotten laid regularly. A *gringa*—white lady. *Guera*—blonde. Not too terrible old. OK, OK!

All the tequila he can drink—*reposada*—the best. All the *filete, chiles en nogada, huitlachoche* he can eat. Fiestas in the fancy houses of the rich, art openings in palacio galleries, his *guera* on his arm. Now and then he spots a compadre with the same good deal.

Angelito is jealous. Naturally. He cruises along *Insurgentes* in his taxi, hoping to see Jane. He begs Jane for work. She lets him paint the exterior patio wall. Brazenly he tries to steal Jane from Chucho. He croons *Aquellos ojos verdes* to honor her green eyes.

Jane is too busy to notice. Jane is a volunteer's volunteer. She helps choose worthy candidates for university scholarships, donated by the *Biblioteca*, to those young Mexicans who are poor but smart. *Gringos* have given enough money to the *Biblioteca* they founded to provide two hundred scholarships a year.

Sadly, neither Chucho nor Angelito would qualify. Jane is aware of the irony. But as many older *gringas* know, they themselves are greatly desired by young working class men. For sex and easy living. Can they do as well at home?

Angelito tries a new tactic. He accuses Chucho of going soft, becoming an old lady's pet Chihuahua. How can Chucho so easily forget their great youthful ambition?

Being macho—*por Dios,* as macho as Angelito—Chucho is ashamed. He once drove a taxi. He once worked out and got the occasional wrestling gig. The two boys generally wrestled each other, alternating winners. When they were found out, sigh, that ended it.

No more husband, says Angelito, we've got to hit Señora Jane. Steal everything in the house. Bring a *camión*, haul it to Señor *Valla*, the fence. Take all her money and head for *El Norte*.

Jane's money is invested at Allen W. Lloyd. She has maybe fifty dollars in casa.

But Chucho *no es tonto*. Angelito, he says, I am going to give you Señora Jane part of the time. You can be her lover on the side.

I doubt it, says Angelito.

It takes Chucho months to convince Jane that Angelito is so jealous he wishes to kill Chucho, his old buddy, to get to her. If she'll only, well, give him some now and then, this will pacify his rage.

Jane pretends this is an awful idea. But it grows on her. Before long, Jane has Chucho as her Significant Other and Angelito as her *casa chica*. With her extra energy bouncing back and forth, Jane works twice as hard at the *Biblioteca*.

Now Chucho is jealous of Angelito, who preens. Chucho cleans off his old neglected *pistola* and loads it. Angelito also wants sole possession so he too finds his gun and loads it up. He hates to dispose of his old compadre from boyhood, but—what can you do? You have to move on in life.

Jane bounces home from the *Biblioteca* and hears a gunshot echo through her elaborate *sala*. What on earth? Then another. Jane finds her S-O and her C-C facing each other with smoking *pistolas*. They both missed.

Put down those guns, you *tontos estúpidos*, Jane hollers, advances and grabs first one then the other *pistola*, which the boys surrender with limp arms. Now, embrace, she orders.

Chucho and Angelito clutch awkwardly and pound each other's back, then face Jane proudly with their arms around each other's shoulders.

But Jane also *no es tonta*. One day she doesn't come home from the *Biblioteca*. Jane is gone. She sold the house right out from under them.

When the new owners arrive, they find Angelito and Chucho in residence. The husband screams at the wife and she screams at him about this appalling situation. It takes awhile but the *policía* get them out. The boys depart with copies of every key in the house.

Now, at last, they stand a chance at their grand ambición to be Hit Men. It just depends on which one wants to get rid of the other most.

Passing by a week later, the quarrel is so loud the boys hear it half a block away. *Ahora!* says Chucho. *Perfecto,* agrees Angelito, who opens the door quietly with their keys.

Husband bellows, wife screams. They do not see the boys.

The boys tiptoe into the *sala*.

They see the boys, go silent.

Chucho aims at the husband. Angelito aims at the wife. Both boys shoot and miss.

Everybody freezes then the couple shrieks.

Chucho and Angelito run out the door, race for Chucho's taxi, *corre corre por la Flecha Amarilla,* and hop on the bus to Dolores Hidalgo.

Ay, Chihua–, huffs Angelito. I have an aunt there.

Policía bustle into the *sala* where *la pareja*, the couple, are stunned and point to bullet holes.

But they missed! say the *policía*.

After a week or so the boys return and go back to their rented taxis. Both cruise the streets searching for Jane. Finally they admit, but not to each other, they are in love with Jane. Jane, that smart *gringa vieja*.

Eventually Angelito gives up. He gives free rides home to a hardworking *chica*, who has a real job as an office clerk. Now they're married and he drops her off at work. He sighs for his luck, his *buena suerte*, as she clicks her heels smartly striding along the flagstones in her pants suit.

Chucho cruises the streets still seeking Jane who was, after all, his first love.

Tiny Tales — 2000 to now

Mascha Beyo

Five feet tall retired Danish ballet dancer Mascha Beyo taught dance and exercise classes at Bellas Artes, the national arts school. Gravel-voiced Mascha, nimble as a girl, toked black Gauloises at age eighty. She was gay and married to George, retired Danish theatre director. Mascha asked him for a divorce and he fainted at her feet.

George got interested in Peggy, retired schoolteacher, and Mascha encouraged them. Either Peggy said no or George wouldn't go. When George finally died, that night Mascha went to a party and said, "George couldn't make it."

At eighty-five with cancer, Mascha was placed on a dais atop a decorated float and paraded around the *Jardín* for *Día de* Mascha, to celebrate all she'd done for San Miguel. She had never accepted a *peso* for the twenty years of classes she expertly taught.

The Lucky Thief

Orchidea stole money and jewelry. She lost three jobs in a row. The *gringo* couple had a false book made to hide their mad money because they suspected she could open safes.

161

Elverado, her husband, was the most skillful beloved gardener-maintenance man-cum virtual manager in town.

Orchidea found the book and took the money. When accused, she demanded a fingerprint expert.

Several of the victimized couples decided to sit down with Orchidea and Elverado, really to seek his help, because they liked Orchidea. She was a good *criada*.

When they told Elverado that Orchidea, his wife of twenty years, had stolen from them, he burst into tears. Orchidea denied it. Elverado cried and cried as hard as a boy. Orchidea comforted him. The couples were ashamed.

Now Orchidea is known as *La Problema*. Couples who hire them change the locks on their safes every couple of months. Elverado is so dependable they can't do without him.

Cowboy & Cowgirl

*T*he Texas couple was so old they almost creaked. He dressed in white cowboy duds. She wore a frilled white cowgirl skirt, fancy gold satin blouse. They perched at a high round cocktail table at Harry's Bar, she cuddling Flossie, her tiny white poodle done up in tiny white fringed skirt and tiny cowgirl hat. Flossie was a recognized star.

Next week was Flossie's birthday. Harry said, "Let's have a party and invite all the local poodles." Sixty poodles and their enamored owners attended the party for ice cream and cake and champagne and doggie delicacies. Everyone barked and had a grand time and Harry laughed and made moolah.

He left her for a young *Mexicana criada* with a child. Any poor young Mexican maid will marry any old *gringo*, 'tis said, because they spend more money in a year than she can earn in a lifetime. And then, the child's father probably refused to marry the mother. And when the nice old *gringo* dies, she may even inherit. Call it win-win.

His wife, they say, is inconsolable.

Pepe

Pepe the parrot holds long intimate conversations with Beto, the crippled gardener at the hotel. Pepe loves Beto who talks to him during planting, raking, cutting and makes Pepe feel his life. Erendia, the owner of the hotel, fired Beto. Probably he leaned on his rake to wipe his sweaty brow, perhaps even to rest, *por Dios*.

That night Pepe the parrot screamed for Beto.

All night long Pepe screamed, "Beto, Beto." Erendia the owner couldn't sleep.

For twenty-four hours Pepe screamed for Beto.

Erendia re-hired Beto. All is serene.

Entrepreneurs

Photojournalist Sue Beere, who took my Authors Photo, works with *Jóvenes Adelantes* which grants college scholarships to smart local teenagers. Sue has been editor of *Atención* four or five times.

Lucina Kathmann runs San Miguel PEN and is now a vice-president of International PEN. Wim Coleman and Pat Perrin run PEN Scholarships for extremely poor school kids.

Nadine Goodman and husband Alejandro Gonzalez began CASA, Mexico's own Planned Parenthood, which gives degrees in Midwifery, and built a hospital for the poor.

Tom Sawyer, retired owner of radio stations, started the summer Chamber Concert Series which brings the Ying Quartet, the Emerson, and Petersburg Piano Trio to town.

Sara Hoch created the film festival, *Expresión en Corto*, which features international short films and documentaries every summer.

ALMA, the old folks home for the poor, was set up by local Mexican matrons.

María Corvarrubias Williams organized Feed the Hungry which operates kitchens in all the little *pueblitos* and schools in the campo to feed 3000 poor daily.

The Asian couple, the Lims, set up a Wednesday feeding program, SOME—So Others May Eat—for two hundred poor people in town..

Lucha Maxwell and Debbie Stein set up *Crecimiento de Niños* for handicapped children. Lucha's disabled vet husband is in a wheelchair. American Debbie was born blind.

Foreigners who live here on money they earned back home—who do not work—feel they owe Mexico for the privilege and do more charitable work than I've ever heard of anywhere. But so do the locals.

Paradise Comes of Age

"What's happening in paradise?" I phoned my buddy Faye from New York. "A serial rapist? It's been on nighttime news, BBC radio."

"Five women," Faye said, "two of them friends. He goes for older *gringas* who live alone, he stalks them. The last one was Jane, three weeks ago."

"Jane! My darling Jane. How is she?"

"She's in the new General Hospital. He—he slashed her. She'll be home this week."

"I'll see her right away. Take care, Faysie."

"You bet, babe."

"Brady and I fly down on Thursday. See you at the hotel on Friday for *comida*."

"We'll be there."

Jane lived on a block of pastel one-story houses, connected and deep, each with one or two patios. Once he got on the roof of the first house, it was dark and he almost fell into the patio. No one was there. In the kitchen he grabbed a butcher knife and climbed back onto the roof. The roof continued to the end of the block with only a foot-high concrete ledge separating the houses.

Jane said this is what he told her. There were dark patios like closed vaginas and softly lit patios like welcoming vaginas. He looked down into the lit patios and when he saw Jane reading on her bed, he knew she wanted him.

When I visited Jane, she was sitting up in bed with a bandaged chest and back, face bruised and puffy. "Angel, what happened?"

"I fought back, even though he stabbed my back. I went crazy."

"I read in the paper they found you passed out on the floor—"

"Bloody, covered in blood." It wasn't easy for Jane to talk. "I'm lucky to be alive."

I hugged her lightly. "But you're not pregnant?"

Jane tried to smile. "Too old, *gracias a Dios*." Jane paused and breathed heavily. "No one got pregnant and no one got AIDS."

"I brought hot empanadas *de atún*."

"My favorites." Wiping tears, she bit and chewed carefully. "Chucho—I should've let Chucho stay with me. He was the one I cared about."

I caressed her arm. "I liked Chucho, Jane."

"He would've protected me. I was so alone ."

This is what Jane said she wants me to put in *Atención*, the paper, to warn other women. The names of all the victims have been in the paper. She signed her name to the article and told me this:

He caught me on my bed and fell on me, one heavy arm pressing my waist, the other over my mouth as I screamed. I bit his hand and he slammed his fist into my head and pushed me down. He was huge, square, brown, muscular, unseeing bullet eyes—and he rammed his heavy body on top of me, one arm pinning both of mine over my head. I began to kick and push, I couldn't scream because his hand jammed my mouth. He stunk. Then I saw the knife and I fought and shrieked, rolled and tried to get my legs off the bed.

"*Quieta, puta,*" he growled.

He slashed my back with the knife and I was paralysed. Waves of terror crashed through tears so I couldn't see straight.

"*No mueve o te corto!*" He tied his kerchief over my mouth.

He jerked down his pants and mine and stabbed me with his penis. Like a knife that missed then cut and stabbed again, his whole violent weight bearing down on me like a tank. Head rolled from side to side, wept and choked, arms shook under his crates of arms, the pain unbearable, then he flipped me onto my stomach, so petrified I got numb, numb, thank God, as he stabbed my anus and finally came all over me. Blood spewed all over from my back.. I knew I was dying.

He rolled me over.

"You made eyes at me on the street," he leered. "*Como te llamas?*" He removed the gag and I spat out blood. Shivvered, shook like a leaf. "*Tu nombre?*" Slammed his paw across my face.

"Ángeles, María de los—"

"Ángeles, tell me about you, Ángeles. I knew you wanted me."

He liked to talk to the women after, according to the newspaper, then rape them again, and talk again and promise to come back soon. And warn them not to call the police, or else he'd come back and kill them next time. I was too far gone to speak.

"You have everything," he said, looking around at the house. He jammed the knife into the sheet and roared laughing at my fear. Wiped it off on the bedclothes pulled up his pants put on his jacket and climbed out the way he came in, by the patio. I passed out.

We made enough racket so my neighbor called the *policía*. Jane stopped and closed her eyes and just breathed. She went on.

A policewoman and man collected my sheets and bedding and took me to the hospital. They worked fast to staunch the blood. His knife slash was bloody but not deep.

DNA was extracted, they treated me for infection, bruises and cuts, lots of antibiotics. I swallowed my morning-after meds. They put me to bed there at the hospital. I was there three weeks till now. The *Cruz Roja* ambulance brought me home. A hospital nurse had cleaned the place and she stayed with me.

"Put it all in, Alicia." Jane was exhausted.

I sat with her for an hour and stroked her arm.

There was a thomping desperate knock. It was Chucho.

"Oh, Jane, Jane!"

"Chucho, at last. Chucho." They fell together weeping.

I left quietly.

Faye and Teo read Jane's rape ordeal in the paper. "Such bravery," Faye wept.

When they got tired of renting in San Miguel Faye and Teo bought a house, early on before prices skyrocketed. A house in a garden enclave right in *el centro*, as they now say, They got married when their daughter, Miranda, was six and they came every summer. They paid forty-thousand; it's now worth add-a-zero. *El centro*—at least four hundred thousand. This town is now a real estate boutique.

Finally they've retired from New York, now Miranda is off to Stanford, and become fulltime artists, at last.

"Probably too late, Fe, but we're as good as anyone here."

They're having shows, their work sells. Several rich couples are collecting them. Life is total *belleza*.

"I'm so proud of you two," I said.

"Let's pray for Jane," said Teo.

Jane's article, the latest in the rape news, caused a ruckus. Vanessa, now elected Judge in San Antonio, which is Baer County, alerted the FBI. The FBI came down and collected his DNA to test and discovered he'd escaped from jail in the States. Now his photo is on TV and in the paper and on bulletin boards everywhere. The rapist is an ordinary working class Mexican in his stocky fifties, a man with so little of interest in his square visage that you wouldn't notice him if he were standing in front of you. He has a mustache as they all do.

It quieted down. He must know they're after him. He must've left town. Three months passed and the town and the older foreign women became less tense.

Vanessa and Faye call me, Alicia, their reformed hippie sex fiend.. They seem amazed that I had consented to that ultimate conventional arrangement known as marriage. But Brady is as wacko as I am. He likes to tote me around on his back and call me his papoose. Now I am married to a practicing Catholic and Vanessa to a lapsed Catholic. Teo and Faith are practicing artists. That's their belief system.

My book on Coatlicue, Deya, and the ancient goddesses; on the Amazons, proved by DNA to have actually existed; on Hildegarde de Bingen, Sor Juana Inéz de la Cruz, and other heroic women is finally finished. It's titled *Ancient Feminists* and it's being published in late fall. My agent says there's already some buzz about it.

They tease me, "Who do you think you are? Christine de Pizan."

"Her *Book of the City of Ladies* was my inspiration," I declare. "Christine is my favorite fifteenth century feminist."

Vanessa and Faye think settling down with Brady calmed me so that my creativity overcame my sexual jumpiness. They forget I've had two novels published.

They caught him!

Policía with FBI caught the serial rapist a week later, hidden right here in town in a cousin's house. They put him in the downtown *cárcel*. He'd escaped jail in Liberty, Texas. As his latest crimes were committed in Mexico, he could not be extradited to Texas. Many photos appeared in the papers and on TV, even in the States. Locals said that had the rape victims been Mexican women, not foreigners, there'd have been no arrests. It wouldn't have made the newspapers. It would not have made the TV. Every year six thousand Mexican women are killed by domestic violence, the most of any country in the world. Six thousand.

As Jane was the latest victim, they asked her to identify him, as the others had. I went with her. She was hidden behind a screen at the jail. "*Sí, es él*. That's the man."

They held him in Solitary for awhile. No interviews were permitted, at first. Some curious men, but no women, went to view. None of the victims who ID'd him wanted to get near him again. Except when the judge held his hearing, they each wished to confront him with their silent rage.

His hearing was held before the Judge with only his victims present. Jane held my hand tightly till she entered the court-room.. I sat outside. They each had to say, Yes, that's the man. The rapist was sentenced to life imprisonment without parole in the new serious jail on the hill above town. So serious and large was the jail that an earthworks was built in front so it cannot be seen from the highway. He got lucky. There is no death penalty in Mexico.

Jane and Chucho moved into a two-story colonial whose roof connects to *nada*. They're both as giddy as teenagers. Jane says Chucho is her lover and the son she never had. He's thirty and she's sixty. He's building a Gaudi-style casa for them with her *moneda*.

The galley of my book just came in the mail. I can't stop look-ing at it. Then the actual book arrived. We all just stare and stare at *Ancient Feminists*, my book finished and published at last, my beloved goddesses and early abbesses and, of course, Christine de Pisan. Wonderful cover of overlapping pre-Columbian god-desses and medieval ladies. Myself, red hair flying, grinning away, on the back cover.

"It's a miracle, baby," says Brady. "You're the genie," I hugged him.

Expat Love

You want me to get pregnant? Ella shouted at Arthur You—you liked my story. His story, published in a literary magazine, was about a childless middleaged man who settled with a woman when he fell in love with her children. But I want my own children. Don't you?

If I refuse you—Ella guffawed—you'll go off with some pobrecita whose husband took off for El Norte? *Una mojada*—wetback—she paddled madly. Just because she has two kids?

Arthur sniffed, Don't you think it's time? Arthur was thirty-six, Ella forty.

The idea grew on Ella but it didn't happen. She got fertility drugs from doctors in San Miguel and Mexico City and in Seattle. Now she'd had her first solo show back home in Seattle, she had time. Her impressionist-fantastic paintings in raucous Mexican color showed lesbian couples, often brown and white, embracing like wood nymphs, standing elegantly and barely touching each other's nipples, as runners, as couples reading, as brown mistress and white maid attracted and about to…. Her sensational show was vilified and praised to the sky, take your pick. Ella had come to San Miguel to be with her *amante*, a Mexicana who dumped her.

173

When Arthur met Ella the lesbian he knew he had to convert her. They went running together, they lifted weights together. They both had tawny skin and thick black eyebrows and wild long hair, so they could pass for Indian. Both were about 5'8", talked and thought the same, and settled here to escape US media culture.

Remember when we were citizens? Arthur said in his fast sardonic voice.

Now we're consumers! Ella boomed and they giggled.

Ella was always in hot water in the gay community because she liked to sleep with men. Arthur's divorced wife had left him for a woman. He'd followed them to Paris and tried being gay but it bored him. Ella was the same Russian-Romanian background as his wife and himself. Only he was Russian Orthodox and she a secular Jew.

Arthur had become a rich young man at twenty-seven when he inherited from his mother, who died early from cancer. Ella arrived with savings from ten years of college coaching that lasted because of the fabulous interest rates in the US and Mexico. Before the peso crashed, 12% a year turned 20K into $2400 which you could live on easily. In 1990 you could still scrape by on $3000. In those days, before money inflated the planet.

Ella liked Arthur because he was good in bed. After a year of horrid romances, she began to listen to Arthur because he seemed to be really in love with her, to *care* about her life. Calling herself a failed lesbian, Ella slowly amazed herself by loving Arthur. Ellita and Arturo became a couple. None of the fertility drugs worked.

Desperate now to get pregnant—having never given it five minutes thought before—Ella consulted with her feminist group in Seattle and they gave her herbs that did work. At forty-two, Ellita was *embarazada*—pregnant—with a healthy baby boy. She decided on natural childbirth which fit both of their *más o menos* New Age sentiments. Husky Ellita kept on teaching *Aeróbicas* and Arturo fairly bloomed with pregnancy. He began holding his hands over his flat belly and sort of jiggling it.

Once Ellita began to round out, Arturo got serious. Feeling her luxuriantly rounded belly, he declared, You understand I'll support our child *forever.*

So?

I'm working very hard on my novel. Up half the night, whenever it strikes me, you understand.

So?

We can't *live* together. Because I have to live *alone.*

Ellita thought he was joking. You built this huge house to live in alone? Ellita lived in a one-room studio.

I'm serious, Ellita. I haven't lived with a soul since my divorce. Arturo looked wild-eyed with fear of distraction.

Turning red-purple, Ellita swung to sock him. Her arm shot out but he backed away fast.

How can you do this to our child? All this was *your* idea. You won't see *me* again! Ellita marched away sobbing.

She was so hurt she ran all the way up the cobblestone hill, a thousand feet up to the top of *Cuesta de San José,* and sat in the field up there and wept and wept.

Brady and I saw her as we climbed to the *Charco del Ingenio,* the high dam above the canyon ravine. I restrained him, "Leave her alone."

Ellita roared and wept. She'd trusted the enemy, a silly phrase she now understood. Before Arturo, men were walking dildoes. She'd toss them away and, ahha, find a new color and shape. Ellita came down from the mountain determined to have their child alone.

When she calmed down, she decided she obviously had to buy a bigger place in a poor neighborhood, something she could afford, for herself and her boy. She struggled not to remain angry because it could hurt her baby. When her stomach tensed with fury, surely her angel boy winced.

She bought an old wreck of a Mexican *casita* on a thin long lot in a Mexican working class neighborhood, whose *ambiente* she loved. She hired a *maestro* to make it livable. During renovations, Ellita made friends with the family next door, a young widowed mother with five children who lived in the house of her *suegra*, her mother-in-law. Her husband had died in his thirties, during a botched kidney operation. Alma, the young *viuda*, worked in a cotton *fábrica* in the house of the *patrón* who was the owner, sewing *camisas y pantalones*.

Arturo would not leave Ellita alone. He hounded her, phoned, appeared around every corner.

Stay home and *write*, she bellowed.

Once—only once—she socked him good. He sprawled in the *calle*. She strode away laughing. Arturo got right up and chased after her.

Here's *moneda*. It must be hard to pay for the house and the studio.

She brushed his arm away, scattering bills.

They screamed at each other on street corners. *Todo el mundo* stopped to watch and snicker. "Vaya, kids," I hollered.

Arturo found it impossible to concentrate on his beloved monolith of a first novel. The novel, titled *Conversions*, was about his from Russian Orthodox to Roman Catholic here in the vibrating soul of the Church, and his devotion to the Virgin of Guadalupe. About his excursion to gay and back to straight, and his attraction to lesbians and women with small children. He'd longed to be—and was now about to be that miracle—a father.

He mooned, head in chin, sighed then straightened up and went back to work. But he dreamed baby, smiling and baby-talking the invisible creature he cradled in his arms. Hating himself, Arturo couldn't write.

Arturo bought baby clothes, crib, walker, every possible *bebé* supply. Soft little blankets, bootees, tiny shoes for ages one month to three years, gowns and rompers and baby boy tops and pants to age three. He spread them out on the sofas in his big *sala* and begged Ellita to come see them.

Don't get near me, she screamed so *los machos* would think he molested her and beat him up.

Please, *querida*, Ellita *de mi corazón*. Arturo all but dragged her to his *casa*.

Ellita ooohed and aaahed, inspecting, and Arturo slung his arms around her and said, I want to invite you to live here with me till our baby is born. To save you money. Let the studio go. Then, when your house is ready…

Ellita lacked the money to turn him down. Plus Ellita wanted calm, no tempestuous anything, so she accepted. I demand a separate bed. You take the guest room, said Ellita, and *bebé* and I will use the master bedroom.

Of course, Ellita. Anything you say.

Hmmph, said she. The only thing I like about this house are the *sanitarios*. At least, they work. Many Mexican toilets are not to be assaulted by tissue except when totally unavoidable. Many deign to flush only by bucket of water poured in.

I'll be a very good father, Arturo promised. I don't have to live *with* you to do that.

Ellita moved in and after a week Arturo moved a cot into her bedroom to sleep near her. Another week passed and she permitted him her bed without privileges of touch. By the third week, ravished with angry desire, they leaped at each other. They resumed their coupledom in such placidity that both forgot about the rift, about everything but the growing arrival, whose urgency they both felt in her belly.

He kicked my hand, Arturo said, and grabbed his own belly.

Sanmiguelenses tittered at Arturo who now ambled the *calles* in his absent-minded way but with his belly thrust forward, holding it protectively with both hands and chatting with it.

After twelve awful hours of labor, Señora Mariana Vélez the midwife alerted Dr. Alvaro, the MD on call. From her athletic years, Ellita's pelvic muscles were too tight for vaginal delivery. Dr. Alvaro performed a Caesarian. Ellita grasped and hugged her wet rosyred baby boy. Back in Arturo's house they lived happy happy happy till Ellita's house was ready.

Then Ellita announced, We are leaving today to go live in my *casita*. This is all yours again.

Arturo's house was big but she didn't like it. It was like rooms built in a well, two dark floors built around a central patio in a box—houses on all sides. There were many dark Colonial box houses in town, one leaning against the next, so the block looked like one solid wall with different colored squares of mismatched heights. Rather like an abstract painting marching down the street. They all had casement windows that opened onto a window ledge balcony protected by iron grillwork. So *niñitos* liked to sit in the windows and watch people on the street.

But, I *don't want you to go*, wailed Arturo.

You should've thought of that, she said in her level sensible way. Before you made me go out and buy a house. Now I'm going to *live* in it.

But my house is too big. *Everything* you need, please, Ellita.

I'm *glad* I have my *own* house where I can do everything *my* way. Ellita had always been ferociously independent.

Tears formed in his eyes. He bent toward her, his hands praying, shoulders swaying, flipping his long hair back and forth.

Sorry, Arturo. She buzzed his cheek, picked up a plastic bag of supplies, adjusted Paco on her hip and left. I'll get the rest later.

As she carried Paco along her new street, her *vecinos* ooohed and aaahed and said *Felicidades* on Paco's safe arrival. *Qué bebé precioso! Niñito adorable!* Ellita already knew the whole neighborhood. She held Paco facing forward *en la moda Mexicana* so he could greet and be welcomed into the human community.

No sooner was Ellita inside her new house than Arturo appeared with more baby stuff. They packed away and put everything in proper order. Ellita's simple one-story house had various rooms facing a long thin open patio with trees, and dirt the gardener was rapidly turning into grass and flowers. Ellita had a maid and gardener, like everyone else in town. Till you hire help, needy folk will knock on your door. *Si no tienes criada, eres criada*, the Mexican saying goes: if you don't have a maid, you *are* a maid.

After two more trips in his car, Arturo had brought absolutely everything. As she put things away rapidly, he kept moving them and stalling.

Thanks, Arturo. She quickly kissed him goodbye.

Arturo started crying as she urged him out the front door and locked it. He banged on the door, wailing, but she ignored him.

Within an hour Arturo returned with his own overnight bag of clothes and moved in with Ellita. He never again lived in his fancy house.

Till you lived with me, I didn't know how wonderful it could be, said Arturo. Forgive me for being such a selfish fool, such an idiot.

Oaf, ignoramus, she laughed. They put Paco in his soft little crib beside their bed, where they fell into each other's arms for life.

Next door Alma's *suegra*, Doña Antonia, babysat Paco along with Alma's growing brood of five. Paco loved to chase the chickens and play with the tiny piglets in the open dirt yard. The family slept in two square brick rooms and cooked outside on stones. They had an outside toilet and a precious shower stall, and Doña Antonia made sure each child was immaculate. Alma now went running with Ellita and Arturo after work. She and Ellita became best friends.

When Paco was three and Ellita forty-seven, she gave birth to a beautiful baby girl, Marilena. Her neighbor, Alma, was in labor and delivered at the very same time. Alma had gotten pregnant for the sixth time when she was raped by her boss at the *fábrica*. At the age of thirty-three, Alma died in childbirth. Her baby boy survived. Ellita suckled the infant boy along with her baby girl. Next door there was now only one adult, an old grandmother, with six children fifteen and under.

Immediately Ellita took Alma's baby boy home with her baby girl. At Arturo's insistence and her immediate agreement,

Ellita and Arturo formally adopted all six children of their dead *amiga* Alma. Doña Antonia, their grandmother, was astounded and grateful. All but the baby continued to live with Doña Antonia. However, Ellita and Arturo were real parents. They clothed, educated, tutored and loved their six new children. All the children sprawled in the *sala* watching TV and chased each other about the long open patio. There were ceramic *piñatas* for birthdays, each blindfolded child swinging a plastic bat to try to break it open. Candy spilled out to gleeful shouts.

Life was beautiful. Ellita and Arturo felt incredibly blessed that, in spite of their earlier evasions, they had both found exactly what they wanted in life. *Sanmiguelenses* said Ellita and Arturo lived in the Do-Gooders Fast Lane. Always helping somebody. In the *campo* Ellita taught free painting classes and Arturo free English lessons.

Life was so beautiful. Every night Arturo played games with the kids. Ellita organized athletic programs for local schools, painted the changes in her life. Now her canvases overflowed with children, flower-like and scrambling and fighting and grabbing. Arturo's first novel didn't sell so he put it aside and wrote another. His several agents sent it around to the major publishers who wrote they loved it. But it wasn't commercial so it wouldn't sell. Finally they gave up.

But the focus of Ellita and Arturo had changed to their bountiful family. Ellita did continue going to Seattle to paint posters and design sets for human rights activist theater groups there. Arturo translated two Eastern Orthodox volumes into Spanish. Ellita began teaching painting to students in the local *preparatorias*. They integrated into the Mexican community. Most of their friends were Mexican, from the working class to the *altagente*.

When life is so beautiful, must there always be something coming? Arturo at age forty-six contracted melanoma cancer. At the urging of his children, he underwent two horribly painful bone marrow transplants in a top rate US hospital. Each seemed to kill the cancer, to work. But it always returned, or lingered, growing unseeable.

Arturo wanted to live. His life was blessed. He had everything to live for. He had money for everything, for all of them, forever. Being smart, he researched his strain of melanoma completely and knew that he would have to die.

Arturo never showed self pity. He relaxed and Brady and I and all his friends visited and all of us took the time to talk fully about our lives. When he was too sick to sit up in bed, we sat on his bed or lay down beside him and stroked his forehead or his arms. Memories from boyhood. Stories about our families. How we first fell in love. How we finally found each other. What we truly cared about. How different and disappointing and sometimes rewarding our lives had been. What, if anything, we expected of death.

When he was too sick to sit up in bed, Ellita sat on his bed or lay down beside him and read to him or simply embraced and held him for hours at a time. The children crowded around Papá to hug him and chatter with him and weep and beg him to get well. Every night Arturo and Ellita's bed was filled with children, their two beside them, and several others at the foot of the bed.

Determined to stay alive for the First Communion of his little girl Marilena and his darling adopted boy, Jaime, Arturo attended their ceremony in a wheelchair, wrapped in blankets, shrunken and bald with lumpy dark spots from radiation. He loaded up with morphine when the pain was unbearable. But he said, I want to be conscious and aware so I hold off as long as possible.

Every day there's always something I enjoy, Arturo told Ellita, in spite of the pain.

Every night she slept beside him in their bed, with the kids all packed around them. The kids felt that as long as they stayed close, Papá wouldn't leave, Papá would live.

One morning Ellita woke up and Arturo was dead beside her. She kissed him and licked him and hugged him and wept. All the children bawled and wept and hugged Papá. They clumped on the bed around Papá hugging him moaning till he began to turn cold and they knew his spirit had left home.

Arturo died at forty-eight. Alone Ellita raised all their diverse children, all eight of them.

Giggling, each child at age eleven studied birth control at CASA. They whispered and tittered together about the amazing sex info they learned. Peer counselors, girls and boys fifteen to eighteen, hauled their infants to class and said, *No hacen esto,* Don't do this. CASA was started by a *gringa* social worker with three kids married to a Mexican of good family, who was appalled at the high birth rate of the poorest.

I permit no stupid teenage pregnancies, Ellita lectured her brood. I am your mother. I will *not* be grandmother taking care of *your* kids. She made sure they all understood their responsibility. Every child who studies will go to college, Ellita shook her finger and bellowed fiercely. Understand? The rest will go to work at age eighteen. Is that clear?

Yes, *ma'am,* said Marilena and Paco, her two. The others gave her melting sweet smiles.

I'm off to class. The kids buzzed her cheek.

Later, passing a small park near her house Ellita saw her fourteen-year-old, Meche, seated on a bench. On the bench lay a boy with his head in Meche's lap, she stroking his hair and ears as he pontificated about *fútbol*. Ellita scowled, almost yelled. Now and then Meche leaned down and kissed the boy. Local girls court the boys, their trophies.

A week later she spied thirteen-year-old Sarita, strolling in her tight jeans and belly button blouse, with her arm around another boy, kissing his cheek.

At home that night, both girls were severely lectured. If you get pregnant, I will kick you out of the house, said Ellita. I remember when boys and girls dare not kiss in public, when they hovered in the girl's doorway.

Tell us about serenades, said Meche.

When I first came here, they still happened now and then. The suitor, the boy, the *caballero*, because they were back then, hired *Mariachis* and serenaded his *enamorada* like Romeo in front of Juliet's house. If she liked him, she opened her window. If not, the house remained closed and dark.

Oh, Mama, that's so silly, said Sarita.

It's romantic, said Meche.

Meche's daughter was born at sixteen, she married the father at seventeen, and they wetbacked to San Diego at eighteen. Both work, Meche babysitting *niños* of local *illegales* and her *esposo* in construction. Sarita had twins at fifteen, refused to marry the father, started college, went on to medical school and is now a local *pediatrista*. During college, of course, Ellita and Doña Antonia and their longtime *criada* cared for her babies.

Her own children with Arturo, Marilena and Paco, are both in *prepa* in San Miguel and high school in Seattle in Spanish and

English. Like Tarzan through the trees, they swing effortlessly back and forth. Marilena is a competition runner and Paco has already exhibited locally as a young painter.

Some married, some wetbacked to the States, one lived with a *borracho*, one is in college studying computers, another works as secretary to a local official, and the others have babies. Now the *casita* overflows with grandchildren, all ages, adult couples and singles moving in and out, losing jobs, leaving husbands, getting work and going back to husbands, cousins and aunts passing through. No one is ever alone because this is Mexico.

One summer they all decide to walk the *peregrinación* to San Juan de Los Lagos to visit the *Virgen de los Milagros* there, the tiny virgin in her white bridal gown worshipped for her many miracles. One hundred miles along the road with thousands of pilgrims. In her van Ellita catches up to them with food at sunset.

Ellita did it all by herself and now that she's graying but still teaching painting and *aeróbicas,* she feels life is rich, indeed. Ellita is no longer an expat. Ellita is *una abuelita*, a Mexican grandmother.

Look what Arturo left me with, Ellita grins. Without Arturo, I'd never have had a family. Arturo gave me a family.

La Aventura de Aurora

urora came out white. Her younger sister Lolita was brown. Pola, the eldest, was a dark shadow in the back of her saddlery shop. Cristóbal and the young doctor were beige and the two youngest sisters white. Most families, as noted, had married in with the Indians fairly early on. Doctor Lucero was brown and his wife pious Spanish white. But it wasn't color, it was class that mattered. Further north were predominately European settlers and to the south Zapotecs and Mayans.

When the Revolution forced the Church to sell its land, dear papá, Dr. Lucero, bought the farmland behind the Oratorio de San Felipe Neri. Everybody loved ebullient wiggly Dr. Lucero whose famous farmacia lay across from the possibly more famous Iglesia San Francisco with its ornately carved facade. I danced with Dr. Lucero at painter Charlie Pollock's roaring parties. Charlie was Jackson's unfamous brother.

San Miguel was still the Hepatitis capital of Mexico in the '60s. At Farmacia Lucero daughter Aurora jabbed my arm with Gamma Globulin, the pre-Hepatitis shot. Aurora lifted her baby boy from the nurse to introduce him to me. "Don't touch," she warned. *"Chiquito precioso,"* she kissed him.

"He's as beautiful as you are," I said. With her black hair and eyes and caring manner, Aurora was our sainted village doctor. When Aurora was fifteen, dear papá began training her to be the doctor and pharmacist he was. Every day after school Aurora spent at the farmacia till it closed at ten PM. At eighteen she married her first handsome gringo.

Every other day I swam at the cerulean blue fifty square-foot swimming pool Dr. Lucero built on his farmland. At the four changing rooms daughter Lolita and her esposo Pancho sold tacos, their tiny daughter in her carriage beside them. By the time Lolita was eighteen and had a son, as well, papá had built a restaurant, a long rectangle that was all windows facing an outdoor dining terrace. Papá installed Lolita as the chef or cocinera and her mother taught her to cook for crowds. Well, both learned. Mama was shy and small, quiet and devout, mother of seven. We all ate at the restaurant beside the beautiful garden with banana and papaya trees, immense palms, and lilies.

In the late Sixties Papá built a hotel with arched terraces, facing the huge garden. When I stayed there in the early '70s, I was greeted on the terrace by vivacious María de la Luz, Dr. Lucero's mistress. María waltzed me the length of the terrace, warbling *"Ese lunar que tiene, Cielito Lindo...,"* in high glee, laughing and hugging me.

For María, Dr. Lucero bought a two-story colonial nearby. His Casa Chica, sacred Mexican institution, was accepted by the family, who treated María de la Luz as an unplaceable relative.

While I stayed at the hotel in '71, Dr. Lucero had my former architect novio, Fernando, built ten two-story houses in a

cul-de-sac around a garden on one side of the hotel. His new
novia was Tina, a blonde gringa painter. Fernando had not had a
Mexican girl friend since he was sixteen. Fernando, my Otomi,
still appealed to me. "Fernando, why didn't you ever propose
to me?" "Alicia," he said, "you didn't want to marry a man. You
wanted to marry a team." He and Tina ultimately married.

On the other side, Papá had already built ten one-story houses, and a small apartment house with a garden. Everywhere the
grounds were graced with hundred year-old high trees from the
Oratorio.

Papá Lucero was determined to take care of his brood.

Summer of '72 Dr. Lucero and María introduced me to
their two small children there in the hotel driveway. Dr. Lucero
seemed very proud to have sired these tiny tots.

Everybody was very merry, as they headed for the cocina to
show them off.

Aurora hugged me as she bustled along with her new baby
girl. She had divorced the gringo and married a Mexican accountant. "I adore him," she told me. By then Lolita had a third
child, a boy, and had divorced Pancho, an abusive borracho.
Pancho managed to die of delirium tremens at age thirty-eight.

When I next appeared in summer '78, dear Dr. Lucero had
died in his early seventies. He was buried in a vault at *Las Monjas
Iglesia* where the elite rested. The family built a lovely fountain
dedicated to him in the garden at the one-story house enclave.
María was especially distraught. Now she had to beg the family
for work in the restaurant kitchen.

Aurora was distraught because her Mexican husband had
been killed in an auto accident. She and her two niños lived in
a big house on the Salida, the rising street out of town leading

to Querétaro, across the way from the hotel owned by the family of Cantinflas, the famous comedian who starred in "Around the World in Eighty Days." Aurora had a two-story aviary filled with songbirds. She bought various rental houses and several apartment buildings around town. Aurora married another gringo, a geologist working on loan to Pemex. They had a boy.

Lolita married a retired chemist, a man her papá's age. "Benjamín says he is a writer." she told me. Lolita was very proud to have a writer, as everybody respected writers as much as painters. She ran the cocina and lived with her three children in a big house behind the hotel. Benjamín lived in a small apartment at the hotel. Every afternoon she carried his comida to him on a tray and they spent the afternoon together. Lolita spent every morning after desayuno with her mother, who now lived in the big first floor apartment in the small apartment house.

Down in the mouth, Aurora divorced her gringo third husband. Every day she worked at the farmacia from nine to one and from four to ten PM, six days a week. Her oldest boy was now sixteen.

"Alicia," she threw her arms around me, "My son tried to commit suicide! He says he does not want to live in this world. He goes to a good school, he has friends. I've taken him to specialists and they all pat him and say he'll get over it, it's just adolescence. I'm frightened."

"He doesn't know me, at all. Do you want me to talk to him? About the hope in life when you find your heart's desire. Like writing, for me."

Aurora asked him and he laughed. "No," he said, "she isn't inside me. Alicia, I can't get *through* to him."

"Your boy has everything," I said.

"Quizás, no," she said. "I'm sending him to Houston to a special treatment center for suicidal teenagers next month."

The next summer I checked into my room at the hotel for two months before flying to Canada to teach fiction for two weeks at the Toronto Writers Workshop at University of Toronto. I hugged Lolita, owner and chef, her daughter and two sons, plus three *meseras*. Ah, at last! Two blissful months to work on my second novel. The hotel filled with wild artists and intense writers, students and teachers, who stayed all summer, for art's sake! Wondrous! Once everybody settled in, son Diego lent me the office typewriter as they would no longer need it.

At the farmacia, Aurora's eyes teared when she saw me.

"Alicia, preciosa," we kissed cheeks. "My darling boy in Houston—they left him alone for ten minutes and he managed to hang himself. He was seventeen."

"Oh God, how can a child do that? He doesn't know WHAT he doesn't know." My eyes teared. "What can I say and what could you do?"

"Nada," she said. "Nada." She sighed and smiled. "I'm married again, to a wonderful Mexican lawyer, a widower. We have a son, look."

Another adorable bundle. "I'm so glad, Aurora." Aurora was strong.

It was five summers before I returned. When I checked in and hugged Lolita she told me Benjamín had died. "I took the *comida* tray up and there he was on the floor, dead of a heart attack. My good good Benjamín."

"Oh, Lolita," I kissed her cheeks and hugged her. "Where are the kids?"

"In college. All three. Now they all speak proper English."

"How's Aurora?"

"Alicia, Dios mío, her husband was killed in a three-car accident. The second one killed on the highway."

That was number four. Aurora now had a live son and two daughters. As they grew, they all worked in the farmacia. The son was gay and his tall sister towered over him.

"Alicia, tell my daughter Mirasol about my *papá*. Alicia knew him before he died in '73."

So I told Mirasol about her wonderful ebullient *abuelo*. "He loved everybody, he charmed everybody. He was handsome and slim and not tall. Everybody's trusted doctor." I went on and on because I wanted her to feel him.

Aurora and a Texas construction engineer were building a huge apartment complex at what was no longer the edge of town. Maybe forty apartments and a huge park garden and a house in the center for Aurora with an immense aviary.

When Aurora married for the fifth time, she chose an older Mexican *contador* and they had a son. Aurora now had four live children.

As the years passed, my second novel had been published. Brady worked in New York and came down to join me when he had summer breaks.

Lolita, in her tight pink pants suit, glowing with love, married her second gringo, Steve, the retired geologist. Steve and his wife had come to the hotel for years. When they divorced, after awhile he came alone. "One day," Steve told me, "Lolita came up to me and put her arms around me and kissed me." Love, love, love again.

After the honeymoon Steve tried to get Lolita out of the co-cina. But Lolita adored cooking. She was as dedicated as Aurora. "Why don't you try Steve in the office?" I suggested. She did but he couldn't handle it. He sat in an easy chair in the cocina and watched her cook, along with the meseras. The waitresses were all assistant cooks.

"One evening," Lolita said, "Steve drove Aurora and me to the top of Atascadero hill to see the sunset. We both burst into tears. Neither one of us had seen a sunset since we were fifteen and beloved papá put us to work."

At sixteen Aurora's youngest daughter, Lola, fell for the weightlifter, Rolfe, a brawny egotist who rode around on his motorcycle flexing his muscles, glaring at the world. Aurora set up Rolfe in a gym so he could support her Lola and their twins. Rolfe ran his scruffy gym and there was talk about drugs. One day folks were working out on the machines when two *pistoleros* charged in demanding money. Calmly, Rolfe handed them bills and said, "Keep on working, folks. They're gone." Being gym fanatics paying by the month, they did.

Lola had a face lift to hold his dulling interest. Rolfe came out as gay. He was kidnapped because of Aurora's money. The ransom was paid and he's back, as full of b.s. as ever. But then it turned out the kidnap rumor was false. There had been kidnap-ping rumors for fifteen years. They were like ghosts that drifted through town. Nobody who saw them would talk. Rolfe decided he was not gay. He was straight. That's where the money was.

After Aurora and her contador had been married almost ten years, he died of a heart attack. Five, Aurora had now lost five. She gave her big house on the Salida to her gay youngest son and moved into her new house in her new apartment development.

Her rental apartments filled fast as they were priced right and todo el mundo trusted Aurora.

Customers asked her for drugs with narcotics she couldn't get. Till brother Cristóbal, who lived with his third wife, second Mexican, on the family rancho, suggested he fly his Cessna to Texas and procure them. How? Leave that to me, said Cristóbal. He landed two small loads at the rancho. His wife wanted a divorce and threatened to turn them in unless he gave her the settlement she demanded. He did. The rancho remained in the family. The poca aventura ended. I put it down to Aurora's grief.

Cristóbal married Maggie, his second gringa, and they went to Laredo to manage the mobile homes she owned that covered a square block of valuable downtown. Her tenants were Mexican families who loved Cristóbal. When the city tried to take Maggie's land, Cristóbal went on TV. He played his guitar and sang *rancheras*. He was so popular in Laredo he could've run for mayor.

But he missed getting drunk at the *Cucaracha* and came back to San Miguel. One morning he phoned Chucho the owner and said, Come open the bar. Chucho said, Cristóbal, can't you wait till noon ? Cristóbal said, I fell asleep behind a table and I need to get *out*. Then he phoned sister Aurora to bring him a fresh suit so he could emerge as a gentleman. This was everybody's favorite story.

Cristóbal's beauty queen daughter from his first marriage divorced her lawyer husband and became a network news host in the big city of Leon. She became a city official in San Miguel, once she'd stopped boozing with her dad.

Aurora's tall daughter and her MD husband moved into the rancho with their darling baby girl. She still worked parttime with her mother in the farmacia. She drove her four-year-old girl into town to kindergarten every morning. Mirasol had a monumental temper to match that of her husband, who as a proper Mexican macho felt it his sacred right to be tyrannical. One morning they had a terrible fight, he took off in his car, and she put her little girl in her car to drive into town. Mirasol was so furious, so tear-filled, that she hit the highway, pulled out to pass without looking, got hit head-on by a truck and killed. The small girl survived. Aurora had now lost two husbands and one daughter to highway accidents.

Almost once a month, shocking news of another car crash death. Mexicans routinely pull out to pass on two-lane roads without looking. Then play chicken. Then consider themselves macho if they survive.

Aurora did not marry again. She became the mistress of a retired married Aeromexico pilot. She also became the darling of a rich gringo widower who loved to take her to fancy shops and buy her pretty silly little things, she told me.

"He's so old," I said. "Can he possibly be any good—?"

"Oh no, Alicia," she giggled, "what he likes to do is kiss his baby girl," and she swept her hand across her hips.

Aurora is endless. She's old, she's still beautiful. She could always take care of herself, as dear Papá had trained her to do. The old gringo died and the pilot got old enough to stay at home. We all got older. By now Aurora was the richest señora in town. She'd done it all herself.

We all got older and fortunately, I got older with Brady beside me.

Aurora's children and Lolita's children all have their own children.

Aurora put her arm around me, "Alicia, it seems *Dios* wishes me to spend my old age alone."

"Con la familia."

"Sí, con ellas."

"El milagro de Mexico—sus familias."

the end

CPSIA information can be obtained at www.ICGtesting.com
Printed in the USA
BVOW07s0928051013

332641BV00010B/140/P